HOW TO FIBERGLASS BOATS – SECOND EDITION

OTHER PRACTICAL "HOW-TO" BOATING BOOKS PUBLISHED BY GLEN-L:

"BOATBUILDING WITH PLYWOOD"
"FIBERGLASS BOATBUILDING FOR AMATEURS"
"INBOARD MOTOR INSTALLATIONS"
"HOW TO BUILD BOAT TRAILERS"

FOR FREE BOOK LITERATURE, WRITE TO:
GLEN-L MARINE DESIGNS
9152 ROSECRANS
BELLFLOWER, CA 90706

HOW TO FIBERGLASS BOATS
SECOND EDITION

BY

KEN HANKINSON, NAVAL ARCHITECT

PUBLISHED BY GLEN-L MARINE DESIGNS

TABLE OF CONTENTS

PART 1

CHAPTER 1

Introduction

As it has been more than a decade since the first edition of this book was written, much information has naturally changed or requires modification. Hence the need for this second edition. Some aspects of the subject have changed in a gradual, evolutionary way, largely through the result of user feedback and experience over time. Other aspects have changed in a more revolutionary way. For example, we'll consider the development and refinement of suitable epoxy resin systems that expand the scope of the subject greatly beyond that of the original text.

Yet the basic application procedures and fiberglass materials themselves are pretty much the same, although some new and even "exotic" materials warrant discussion. Thus if you've read the first edition of this book, you'll find much that may be familiar. However, there's considerable new information presented. Because of the context of the many new options and choices now available, the text has been completely rewritten, revised, and updated to be as current as possible in a field that is ever-changing. You'll find much valuable information whether you are building a new boat, restoring or repairing an old boat, or even if you are not working on a boatbuilding project and instead are using the materials in other applications.

Basically, the subject of the book is how to cover or sheath boats with fiberglass when used in conjunction with various types of resins. Yet these materials have many other uses. Thus the information presented may be considered as a handbook to using these materials in a variety of applica-

tions, with perhaps some minor modifications on the part of the user to suit his specific requirements. While this is a practical "how-to" book, enough technical information is thrown in where necessary to explain the topic, and perhaps adapt the data to your needs, but in such a manner so as not to boggle the mind.

In the first edition, the book included some ancillary chapters relating to actual fiberglass boat construction and so-called "one-off" fiberglass materials and methods. These chapters have been largely deleted or revised for several reasons. First, these subjects really do not apply to sheathing processes directly as such. Secondly, in view of the fact that the book should be kept brief for easy reading and remain reasonable in price, there simply was not room. Finally, the subject of "one-off" fiberglass boat construction from the standpoint of the amateur boatbuilder is so broad in scope that it requires its own book; for those interested, "FIBERGLASS BOAT-BUILDING FOR AMATEURS" was written by the author.

The style of this book has been kept informal and therefore (it is hoped) easy to read and follow. Keep in mind that this is a field of fact, fiction, and opinion, and any author does his best to interpret which is which. While much of the material presented is based on the author's personal experience, of greater importance is the fact that the text is a compilation of experience based on generations of feedback from countless amateur boatbuilders gathered through the auspices of GLEN-L Marine Designs, one of the largest suppliers of boat plans, kits, and fiberglass supplies in the amateur boat-building field. In addition, considerable testing and research was done and data gathered from other designers, product manufacturers, suppliers, and technical people in the field.

The reasons for writing this book are several. Not only will most amateur boatbuilders include fiberglass in at least some portion of their project, but those who own boats may want to make repairs or restore old boats, and will invariably consider fiberglass (rightly or wrongly) to help solve their problems. This is where the questions, opinions, and even controversy, cause much confusion leading to wasted time, effort, and money. The purpose of this book is to sort things out for all involved in these types of projects and provide the correct information needed.

Yet much controversy and differing opinions still exist on the subject; no book, no matter how up-to-date, can be expected to resolve them all. Even though considerable testing and research was done in writing the book to resolve conflicting information, resolving controversy is NOT the goal. What IS the goal is to enable the reader to select the proper combination of materials to do the job, work with them as easily and safely as possible, obtain satisfactory and durable results, and avoid pitfalls.

Of primary importance in realizing these goals is taking some of the fear and anxiety out of the task and dispelling some of the myths. While failures certainly can occur, one prime purpose of this book is to tell you how and why such failures can occur so you won't have to suffer through them. Furthermore, where a failure or potential for same may occur, information will be presented to make a fix.

If you have no experience at all with fiberglass, or your experience is limited,

most of the information presented will be useful. Even if you have considerable experience, you'll probably find much that's new or something that you may not have thought of before. While the term "fiberglass" has been used up to this point in a generic way, other similar materials will be presented and discussed which offer alternative, but similar, ways to solve problems facing the boatbuilder or owner working on his boat.

In fact, there are many possible combinations of fiberglass and related materials to use on boats of varying types and methods of construction, and the strengths and weaknesses of these possible combinations will be explored. So whoever you are, whatever the boat in question is, hopefully a result that satisfies your requirements will occur, along with a valuable learning experience. If you derive pleasure out of the work, as most do, so much the better. Best of luck on your project.

NOTE: Care in use of the materials to be discussed is important for personal safety, and the reader should look over the chapter on "SAFETY" carefully before using any of the materials, as well as read all the precautions on the labels of products to be used. Even the experienced user should review this material since much information includes new thinking on the subject. Because many of the photos in the book have been taken over time and may come from several different sources, some of the practices inadvertently shown may not include proper safety precautions in all cases. For example, some photos may show a worker not wearing proper hand or skin protection. Nevertheless, the reader should consider and heed all safety warnings and follow instructions to the letter.

CHAPTER 2   Why Cover A Boat With Fiberglass?

It may seem self-evident why one should want to cover a boat with fiberglass. But the surprising thing is that many people do not realize the REAL reasons. Some just assume that it's the thing to do because they've seen it done before. Others have misconceptions as to what the product can do. For example, many novices consider the fiberglass sheathing to be a "wonder" material that will cure all future ills.

Unfortunately, much of the misconception surrounding fiberglass sheathings is the result of promotional efforts and false information passed on from those with vested interests, i.e., the people who want to make a buck selling the materials. The primary reasons for covering or sheathing a boat hull with fiberglass, however, are quite basic, and are as follows:

1. Reduce hull maintenance
2. Improve appearance
3. Keep water out of the boat
4. Protect the hull from impact and abrasion.

These are the REAL reasons, and any ONE of the above may be reason enough to go through the work and expense of doing the job if you think your boat is worth it. Of course, there can be secondary reasons, the importance of which will vary considerably depending on the type of boat, the waters in which it will be used, and the service to which it is put.

For example, you can add new life to an old boat by covering the hull with fiberglass (assuming it is of suitable construction, as will be discussed in Chapter 8). This can often add some strength and watertightness to the seams and joints, as well as reduce moisture absorption which adds unnecessary weight to a boat. Or you can use fiberglass materials for repairing or restoring old or damaged parts within the boat, thereby extending its useful life. Or you might cover a new boat with fiberglass materials just to protect it from marine parasites such as shipworms or teredos, or rot. In all cases, the smooth fiberglass surface reduces resistance and drag underway, adding to fuel economy.

One of the biggest misconceptions that the novice has is that a fiberglass covering will add considerable strength to a hull. However, while partly true, generally this is a fallacy. The fiberglass covering, which usually utilizes cloth and resin, should be considered as a non-structural protective or cosmetic covering only. For this reason, the boat owner should not be misled into thinking that he can take a structurally weak or unsound hull, slap some cloth and resin on it, and make it sound, or reduce planking thickness and make up for it with a fiberglass covering. Such an approach is usually doomed to failure.

Few realize it, but fiberglass on a weight basis does not have nearly as much stiffness as does wood for example, and is in fact quite flexible. Thus there is no practical way a thin layer of fiberglass can "stiffen up" a hull that may be flexing, especially if the flexing is caused by an unsound structure. There are some approaches to restoring older boats with fiberglass, however, as described in Chapter 14, but these consist of more than a lightweight, thin sheathing, and are much more involved than a simple sheathing application.

Probably one of the most repeated claims about fiberglass (whether for sheathing uses or as applied to the factory-built all-fiberglass boat) is that "you'll NEVER have to paint your boat again, EVER!" This statement is ONLY true if you don't care what your boat looks like!

It IS true that the resin coating used with the material, as well as the resin gel coat (outer coating) used on factory-built fiberglass boats are finished surfaces in themselves that offer some degree of protection. However, even though the gel coats on factory-built fiberglass boats contain a "molded in" color, and resin can be pigmented in covering work applied over other types of boats, such surfaces still need the protection of a paint system or other

This plywood planked boat was built by an amateur who had never built a boat before. The entire hull was covered with a single layer of fiberglass cloth and clear polyester resin. The natural finished foredeck of ribbon grained mahogany was covered with lightweight deck cloth without staining the wood beforehand. The entire boat was finished with a sprayed two-part epoxy paint system for a rich, deep finish, using a clear finish on the foredeck. The resulting hull will be maintenance free for many seasons.

specialized coating. If not protected, they will sooner or later fade, lose their color intensity, become "blotchy" with atmospheric exposure, or perhaps "chalky", and generally become unattractive from the normal scrapes and bumps all boats are subjected to.

In fact, one of the bigger problems that has developed with surfaces of many factory-built fiberglass boats (at least below the waterline) is a phenomenon known as gel coat osmosis, an unsightly blistering and pockmarked appearance that can lead to extensive and expensive repairs. In short, just about all boats will require surface protection and periodic recoating with paint or other coating systems to enhance or restore their original appearance, depending on the extent of exposure and use.

What IS true about the fiberglass sheathed boat as opposed to the boat without a sheathing is that in most cases the boat will probably go two, three, or more seasons without needing paint. This is quite an improvement over old uncovered wood boats which require a fresh coat of paint each season. Paint coatings last considerably longer when applied over a substrate that's made more stable by the fiberglass sheathing. Of course, for boats that remain in the water all season, a special anti-fouling bottom paint is still required in most areas on ANY boat regardless of what it is made from.

In short, whether the boat is made from all fiberglass or is covered with fiberglass materials, it WILL require maintenance, but probably NOT at the rate of boats made from other materials, or those NOT otherwise protected by fiberglass sheathing. Furthermore, it will be cheaper to maintain overall, and such maintenance will be easier when it is required. This is especially the case when one of the suitable epoxy resins is used in the fiberglass sheathing application.

As can be seen by photographs of some of the boats in this book, a covering of fiberglass cloth and resin can do wonders for a boat's appearance. Of course, this applies only when the job is done correctly according to the methods specified in this text, and assuming that exposed surfaces are painted or coated with a suitable product or system applied per the manufacturer's instructions. To achieve success, FOLLOWING THE INSTRUCTIONS PROVIDED WITH THE PRODUCTS YOU WILL USE THROUGHOUT THE FIBERGLASS APPLICATION CANNOT BE OVEREMPHASIZED!

Generally speaking, the manufacturers of resins and paints or coating systems spend a considerable amount of time, effort, and money in testing and research to develop products which will give good results when used properly. By not following instructions, you'll probably wind up with a boat that may actually look WORSE than it did before it was covered with fiberglass.

The combination of fiberglass and resin forms a seamless envelope around the hull which effectively keeps water from passing through seams or joints and into the boat, assuming such joints are structurally sound. This same capability can be put to good use on decks and cabin tops to keep water out of the accommodation spaces on larger cruisers, and in the case of wood boats, this can halt significantly the promotion of rot in the process.

Now that you know some of the REAL reasons for covering a boat with fiberglass, you can better decide if your boat should be covered and why you'll be doing it. You'll have to weigh the benefits of the covering, both with regard to the value of your boat as well as the cost and effort required to do the job. Because of the several combinations and options available in both the resins and sheathing materials that can be used, you'll need to know more about these before you can make an informed choice, and that's what will be covered in the following chapters.

CHAPTER 3   Fiberglass Materials

The terminology "fiberglass" has virtually become a household word. Because the term is so common, and to keep things simple, it will be used in a generic way throughout most of this text. However, there are materials other than so-called "fiberglass" that can be used for sheathing which warrant separate discussion elsewhere in the text. For certain applications and uses, these other materials and their application processes may offer different or unique qualities not possible with true fiberglass. The reader should review these alternatives, in addition to the text on true fiberglass materials and methods, so that the proper choices can be suited to his particular application. Therefore, keep in mind that the so-called "fiberglass" sheathing process may not be the ONLY solution to a sheathing problem.

WHAT IS FIBERGLASS?

True fiberglass materials and the composite products made from them have suffered from an abundance of names that, quite simply, refer to the same thing. Depending on the geographical area or who is talking, one might hear terms such as "glass-fibre", or "glass reinforced plastic", or "GRP", all of which are commonly used in England and Europe, for example.

Or in this country, one might hear the terms "fiberglass reinforced plastic", "FRP", "glass fiber", as well as the word "fiberglass", in common use. In all cases, these terms mean the same thing, which is the use of fiberglass materials usually in conjunction with some type of liquid plastic resin.

Yet few people know what fiberglass really is. Basically, it's a material made from glass filaments. With the advance of technology, many new types of glass filaments with high strength properties and other specialized characteristics are now available or in the process of development. However, due to economic considerations and the fact that most boats generally need only materials of medium strength with high rigidity, the type of fiberglass filament most often used in fiberglass materials for boat work is technically known as "E-glass", the "E" standing for "electrical grade".

For the technical reader, the actual glass used is a lime-alumina borosilicate glass of low alkali content with a high chemical stability and moisture resistance. This glass composition offers ample properties of flexibility, strength, and abrasion resistance under most marine conditions. Stronger glass compositions are made (such as high-strength "S-glass" which has about 20% greater tensile strength than "E-glass") but are more expensive, and availability of products made from them more limited. Unless added strength properties are critical, materials made with "S-glass" are not necessary in the majority of sheathing applications.

Regardless of the chemical composition, the glass filaments are made into materials known as "fiberglass". These materials include cloth (or "fabric"), various mats, rovings, woven rovings, and specialty materials and fabrics that may combine two or more of these materials into one, or orient fibers in one or more directions in a non-woven format. Most of these will be discussed in greater detail later.

CLOTH

Fiberglass cloth is woven from fine yarns of various twist and ply construction into a wide range of types, weights, and widths. For boat-covering purposes, cloth is usually a plain square open-weave type where the lengthwise and crosswise yarns intersect alternately at right angles, much like a basket weave. This type of weave has the maximum number of interlacings, the most crimp, and the highest stability. Other weaves of cloth (such as satin weave) are available and may be suitable, but aren't as common.

Cloth is categorized by WEIGHT PER SQUARE YARD, ranging from approximately 2 ounces (very light) to 40 ounces (very heavy) per square yard. Cloth thinner than 4 ounces is not durable enough for most boat work, while cloth much heavier than about 10 ounces is more difficult to wet out and form around corners and contours. Generally, the heavier weight cloths are not necessary; heavier sheathings can be achieved by adding more layers of a lighter weight cloth, or adding a layer of mat. Both these approaches will be discussed later.

Lightweight 4- and 6-ounce cloth is often used on the decks of smaller boats, and hence is often called "deck cloth". It is also ideal where a natural wood finished surface needs protection. This light fabric becomes very transparent when wetted out with resin, with the weave becoming practically invisible. This allows the true beauty of the surface below to stand out through the clear resin. For more general covering purposes, such as hull, deck, and cabin top areas, cloths ranging from 7½ to 10-ounce should be used as they offer greater durability and resistance to scrapes and abrasion.

Commonly available widths of cloth are 38″, 44″, 50″, and 60″, usually sold by the running yard. Also available are cloth tapes with selvaged edges in widths from about 2″ to 12″ which are ideal for reinforcement of localized areas and can be applied along seams to help make a boat watertight. While you could cut any fabric up into strips to make your own tape, these strips would not have a selvaged edge and the tendency is for them to unravel. However, this can be overcome and you can make your own tape if desired. Here's how.

Stretch out a length of cloth over a sheet of cardboard using masking tape to hold the material in place. Use a straight edge to mark off widths as desired. Brush along these lines with uncatalyzed polyester resin, which may be thinned up to 10% with acetone for this purpose (an exception to the rule of not thinning resin) using the edge of the brush so as to form a thin bead of resin. This resin edge allows easy cutting while keeping the yarn from unravelling. Let the resin set for 10 to 15 minutes and then cut along the lines with a razor knife. Store the strips of fiberglass cloth tape so formed in an air-tight container such as a plastic bag or box to keep the resin from drying out until used. The tape should be used within a few days as it may become difficult to wet out if the resin bead looses too much of the solvents through drying.

Cloth is the most expensive form of fiberglass material on a weight basis, and thus is seldom used in the production of all-fiberglass boats. If cloth were the primary material used in building such a boat, it would be very uneconomical to use as it takes too much of the material to build up the thickness necessary for strength and stiffness. When cloth is used in fiberglass boatbuilding (and it seldom is), it is usually used in conjunction with various compositions of mat and/or woven roving. Cloth by itself is used almost exclusively for coverings or sheathing work on hulls, decks, cabins, repair work, and similar applications.

BASIC FIBERGLASS MATERIALS

(a) *Roving—Strands of glass fibers are grouped together to form untwisted yarn. The roving is either used in a "chopper gun" or woven to form woven rovings.*

(c) *Mat—Randomly oriented strands of glass fibers forming a bulky thick felt held together with a resinous binder.*

(b) *Woven roving—A coarse fabric made from roving. It resembles cloth but is much heavier.*

(d) *Cloth—Woven fabric made from fine yarns of fiberglass. Two examples shown are a regular 10 ounce cloth, while the finer cloth is a light weight 4 ounce "deck" cloth.*

CLOTH FINISHES

In weaving the fiberglass cloth, the yarns made from the strands of filaments must be protected from abrasion and breaking during the weaving operation by lubricating materials called "sizings" that are not compatible with the resins that will be used later. Hence they must be removed, and a common way to do this is by baking the cloth or burning off the sizing materials. Various chemical treatments or "finishes" are then applied after this heat treatment.

A wide variety of finishes are available to meet many requirements in current fiberglass laminating procedures including sheathing applications, and to suit the wide variety and types of resins available. Basically, the finishing treatment has to do with "wettability, or the time it takes for the resin to saturate the fabric. The finish also improves the adhesion between the glass and the resin, and one type of finish may yield better results in this regard with one type of resin than with another.

There are many types of finishes and each fiberglass weaver seems to have his own "special process" that he claims is "superior" to others. Some cloth manufacturers have indeed developed their own

"hybrid" finishes which may be better than one type of finish alone. But for the cloth fabrics most commonly used in sheathing boats, the "chrome" and "silane" (or "amino-silane") finishes are common and proven. Other terms seen on suitable finishes include "Volan", "Garan", and "Sea-Glass".

From the consumer's standpoint, this makes things confusing, especially since many firms selling fiberglass cloth have no idea what a finish is, let alone what type is used. One cannot tell the type of finish used by appearance; they are all the same in this regard. If you ask many merchants about the cloth they sell, the usual reply is, "we've got boat cloth", which will probably suffice. In any case, these finishes are what give the fiberglass fabrics their characteristic "white translucent" appearance and their ability to be wet out by the resin while bonding to a surface material or "substrate".

This leads to a tip for the unwary: If someone offers you fiberglass material which does NOT have this white translucent quality, or otherwise looks dirty or greasy, or has dark colored streaks, patches, or spots, DON'T BUY IT NO MATTER HOW CHEAP IT MAY BE! Such material may not have been cleaned or finished,

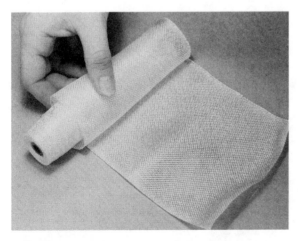

Fiberglass cloth tape is a narrower form of fiberglass cloth and has selvaged edges. Or you can make your own using techniques described in the text.

This close-up shot of fiberglass chopped strand mat clearly shows the random fiber orientation of this material.

or was not finished completely or properly. It may not wet out properly and may prevent bonding of the resin to the surface. Thus it is recommended that if you cannot look at the product before you buy it, select merchants who commonly deal in the materials and won't risk their reputations by selling defective or inferior material knowingly.

MAT

Fiberglass mat is a reinforcing material made from glass fibers about 1" to 2" in length, or continuous strands arranged in a random swirl pattern formed into a felt-like product. The fibers are held together with a dry resinous binder. Because mat is cheap and builds up thickness (and subsequently, stiffness) quickly, it is commonly used in fiberglass boat production, even though it is heavy. The binders used in the mat must be highly compatible with polyester resin (since this is what's commonly used in the factory) in order to wet out the thick, heavy material quickly.

However, the binder may create a problem if other resins are used, especially epoxy resins, which may be incompatible with the mat binders. Thus if you want to use mat with epoxy resin, you must determine that the epoxy being used will wet out the mat being used. Unfortunately, due to the wide variety of epoxy resin formulations, not to mention mats and their respective binders, this may be difficult; some work, some don't. But from a logical perspective, due to the higher cost of epoxy resins, and the greater amount of resin required to wet out mat, there is little justification or need for this combination. Thus, in general, mat and epoxy resin should be avoided if only to conserve materials.

The type of mat used in boat work is commonly referred to as "chopped strand mat" or "CSM", and is categorized by WEIGHT PER SQUARE FOOT (not per

square yard as are cloth and other woven materials). Weights popularly vary from approximately ¾ ounce to 3 ounce per square foot, with 1-, 1½-, and 2-ounce weights most common.

Mat is generally considered the cheapest of fiberglass reinforcement materials on a weight basis, and hence is commonly used. However, mat absorbs a higher percentage of its weight in resin and may tend to be brittle when used alone with resin. Mat is easy to wet out with polyester resin and it gives positive bonding between layers of cloth and/or woven roving while building up thickness. It also shapes readily and can conform to complex shapes easily. Mat, however, is not as strong as cloth or woven roving, and this is why it is commonly used in conjunction with other reinforcing materials; it helps form a laminate with balanced strength and stiffness properties.

Mat is commonly available in 38" and 50" widths and is sold by the running yard or by weight. Because the mat fibers are only held with a thin, dry resinous binder, many loose strands may be apparent. This is not important and does not mean that the mat is defective. Even small holes and voids can be tolerated in the mat without detriment, as once the mat is saturated, it can be pushed and shoved around to some extent to cover over these areas. So don't be too hard on your supplier if the mat you receive looks a little like it's falling apart; that's the nature of the stuff.

WOVEN ROVING

Woven roving (often abbreviated "W.R.") is a coarse, heavy, open weave fabric which resembles cloth fabrics, but usually does not have a selvaged edge. Because of this, there is a tendency for the rovings to pull apart and away from one another, especially along the edges. A few loose strands won't affect the material, but care should be exercised in handling and use so as not to pull the material apart.

The square weave type is commonly used in boat work. Woven roving is made from rovings which consist of continuous strands of glass fibers grouped together to form untwisted yarns or rope-like structures. These rovings are arranged into a lattice or basket-type weave to form the material.

Woven-roving is categorized by WEIGHT PER SQUARE YARD, ranging from approximately 14 ounces to 40 ounces. Commonly used weights of woven roving are 18- and 24-ounce varieties. Widths are usually 38" to 50" and the material is commonly sold by the running yard or by weight.

Woven roving gives strength to a laminate at a cost lower than cloth fabrics, which makes it an important element in fiberglass boatbuilding. But because of its coarse appearance, it is not used where appearance is important, since the weave cannot be concealed without an excessive amount of resin build-up. Furthermore, woven roving is more difficult to wet out than either mat or cloth, and all these elements make it not as suitable or popular for most sheathing applications. The material is often used in alternate layers with mat for fiberglass boatbuilding laminates.

OTHER FIBERGLASS MATERIALS

Cloth, mat, and woven roving are the three primary materials which this book is most concerned with since they are the most common and readily available materials, and their cost is favorable. They are also the most likely materials to be considered in sheathing work. However, there are other fiberglass materials or combinations that may be available which will be mentioned to inform the reader.

One such product is a combination of mat and woven roving made into one material and commonly used in production fiberglass situations where plenty of labor is available. The primary advantage of this product is that it can save time. "Fabmat" and "Stitchmat" are trade names for specific products of this type. The latter material is held together with stitching instead of the usual binder, and thus is said to be compatible with epoxy resins as well as polyesters. However, because of the weight of this product and resulting difficulty in wetting it out by the individual worker, plus the fact that its properties are seldom needed in most sheathing work, it is seldom used, except perhaps in workboat applications.

Other materials include the more sophisticated, and usually costlier, unidirectional, bi-axial, and tri-axial rovings sometimes referred to as "exotic" materials. While these can and are made from all-fiberglass yarns, "hybrid" materials are also available which include other types of reinforcements in them, such as Kevlar and carbon fiber.

The main difference in these specialty materials as compared to conventional woven rovings is that the fibers are usually non-woven and the strands are oriented into distinct and specific directions. This is done so that strength properties can be oriented in specific directions. Because the materials are non-woven, the laminates made from them will be thinner and lower in weight, but higher in strength on a weight basis.

However, these materials are not really intended for sheathing work. They are only slightly better than woven rovings in their poor surface appearance, and more costly than cloth fabrics. Their specific directional strength properties are usually not necessary in the typical sheathing application. However, they could be used for localized reinforcement, e.g. to reinforce seams, and then covered with fiberglass cloth for better appearance.

Fiberglass laminates are a synergetic composition; that is, they consist of two or more materials which work together to develop characteristics that are better or greater than if one of the materials was used alone. One of these materials, the fiberglass (or reinforcing) material itself, has already been discussed, with similar reinforcing materials being discussed in future chapters. The other material in the composition (whether fiberglass or some other type of reinforcement is used) is the resin.

The world of plastics has developed so many different types of resins, with more being added all the time, that it's a wonder the chemists can keep matters straight. However, for sheathing applications, there are only a few basic resin types that are of any current concern; these are the polyester, epoxy, and to some degree, the vinylester types.

These resins are quite different from paints even though polyester and epoxy based paints are available. Paints, in general, are mixtures of pigments suspended in a volatile liquid. When paint is applied to a surface, this liquid evaporates, leaving a dry film containing the pigments. Resins, however, are liquids that react chemically to form solid plastics, and don't "dry" in the manner of paints; they "cure" instead. Thus their performance qualities and application characteristics are completely different from paints.

These three types of resins are classed as "thermosetting" resins; that is, they cure or set up by internally generated heat and cannot be melted or liquified again by the application of heat (unlike a "thermoplastic"

resin). They are not very strong by themselves; however, when combined with a reinforcing material such as fiberglass, strength gains develop quickly.

All these resins are in liquid form initially. However, there are numerous subtypes and formulations available in each of the three types depending on application needs and requirements, and service expectations. NEVER mix any of these three resins together in the uncured or wet state. This chapter will attempt to sort things out by describing their various qualities and characteristics so you can select the proper type to match your sheathing requirements.

POLYESTER RESIN

Polyester resins are commonly used in production fiberglass boatbuilding and also for sheathing. Polyester resin tends to be brittle when unreinforced, and this quality makes them unsuitable for coatings or gluing (unlike epoxies). They are also more subject to moisture absorption than epoxies. Polyesters are petrochemical-based products which begin life in the oil refining process. The following briefly describes how the resin is made; while somewhat technical terms are used, they are not necessary to your knowledge of the products, but substitute words simply don't exist.

In the manufacture of the resin, various anhydrides, polybasic acids, glycols, and styrene are made by reaction processes from benzene, propylene, and ethylene, which the resin manufacture "mixes" together and "cooks" in large kettles or reactors. This cooking process tends to "harden" or polymerize the resin as well as increase the thickness or viscosity.

The cooking process is stopped short (or "half cooked") and then the product is thinned with styrene. Resins used for boat-building and sheathing applications usually contain between 38% and 48% of this styrene. Once thinned with styrene and a promotor added, the resin is ready to be sold. Of course, resin manufacturers can vary the ingredients and formulate resins which are suited to particular applications, and as a result, all polyesters are not the same. Also, various fillers, promoters or accelerators, and other modifying additives may be included for special duty uses.

If the cooking process just described were carried through, the resin would harden completely. But since the process is halted part way through, the resin is said to be "pre-polymerized" or partially hardened. However, because the resin has been sent on its way to eventual hardening, the cooking procedure causes a lasting effect on the resin and it will still eventually harden over an extended period of time on its own, even if cool. This is one reason why polyester resin should be "fresh" when purchased and used, as old resin may not function properly because it may be too close to this eventual cure.

Most resin manufacturers do a good job in assuring that they, as well as their distributors, maintain fresh stock. The useful shelf life stated by most suppliers is from six months to one year, although this can be increased by adding inhibitors or by refrigerated (not frozen) storage. If resin is purchased and not used promptly, it should be stored in a cool, dry place, that will not freeze, but preferably below 70°.

When using resin, the user can't wait forever for it to harden, so to fully complete the polymerization (or cooking) process on demand, or in other words "cure" the resin,

two additional ingredients are required. One is called the "accelerator" and the other is called the "catalyst". These two elements work as a "team" to help the resin speed up its final job. The accelerator and the catalyst produce an internal heat in the resin which makes the final cure or "hardening" possible, and within a reasonable or brief period of time.

For polyester resins used in boat work, the common accelerator used is technically known as cobalt napthanate (commonly referred to as "cobalt"). The usual catalyst is methyl ethyl ketone peroxide. This catalyst is often referred to as "M-E-K" in error since it should be "M-E-K-P". Methyl ethyl ketone (or "M-E-K" without the "P") is actually a solvent in the acetone family and NOT a catalyst at all. NEVER USE THESE TWO INTERCHANGEABLY!

The heat that the accelerator and catalyst cause is the result of a rapid oxidation, the speed of which is determined by the amount of each added, as well as by the ambient temperatures where the curing takes place.

At one time polyester resins were sold without either of these two elements in the resin; it was called "unpromoted" resin. They were added later by the user as required. However, one serious problem developed. It was tragically discovered too often that when cobalt and M-E-K-peroxide were mixed into the resin AT THE SAME TIME, they could catch fire and violently explode due to the immediate, rapid, and uncontrollable release of oxygen created by the coming together of the two materials.

As a result of this experience, resin manufacturers now mix cobalt into the resin (now called "prepromoted" resin) by itself at the factory, and the catalyst is packed separately for final addition by the user. However, because these two items can still be purchased separately by the ultimate user, one important safety rule must be emphasized:

WARNING: DO NOT MIX COBALT NAPHTHANTE AND METHYL ETHYL KETONE PEROXIDE TOGETHER AT THE SAME TIME AS A VIOLENT REACTION OR EXPLOSION WILL OCCUR.

The final addition of the catalyst will make the resin harden by the heat set off by the reaction within the resin. The speed of this reaction depends on several variables. These variables include ambient temperature and the amount of catalyst added (as noted previously), as well as the volume of resin and how it is distributed (concentrated large volumes set up faster than small volumes dispersed over larger areas), and to some extent, humidity. High humidity slows or may even prevent curing, while low humidity speeds curing.

The catalyst is too explosive in its pure form for safety; it is normally in solution with a non-reactive solvent and hydrogen peroxide. Because ratios vary with catalyst manufacturers, some differences in cure characteristics may occur. Thus, interchanging catalyst suppliers within the same batch of resin may yield somewhat different results. A test batch can be made prior to use to check this out if brands of catalyst are changed.

Note that catalyst, too, can lose strength or potency with age, so more may be required for comparable gel times if it is not fresh. Average amounts of catalyst are 1% to 2% by weight, but variations of from 0.5% to 5% will have little ill effect if conditions warrant these variations.

Polyester resin is an air-inhibited resin; that is, the air exposed surface will not cure in the presence of air and will exhibit surface tackiness. In order for the resin surface to cure completely (at least within a reasonable period of time), it must be sealed off from the air. This can be done in two basic ways.

The ordinary way is to purchase a resin that contains a non-air-inhibiter; this is a wax solution built into the resin, or as will be shown in Chapter 9, you can add your own wax solution when you desire this quality in the resin. The wax solution will "float" to the surface once the resin has been applied, thereby sealing out the air and allowing the resin to cure. A polyester resin which contains this wax is commonly referred to as a "finishing resin" because it is usually used as the final coat, allowing the resin to cure solid and tack-free for final finishing and sanding. If multiple coats of this resin are used, each coat MUST FIRST BE SANDED to remove the wax coating before applying another.

The other way to cure the resin is to seal the surface from the air AFTER applying the resin by applying a surface coating over the wet resin. This can be done by using a sheet material such as cellophane, Mylar, plastic wrap, wax paper (all of which are called "parting films"), or by a spray application of a product such as polyvinyl alcohol (known commonly as "P-V-A", a type of "release agent").

Resin which does not contain wax, as does finishing resin, is commonly referred to as "laminating resin". This resin is not used as a last or final coat, but instead allows for continuous applications of additional coats of resin as might be done when building up a laminate. Sanding between coats is not necessary. Therefore, the two basic types of polyester resin most commonly used are:

1. LAMINATING RESIN (AIR INHIBITED, CONTAINS NO WAX)
2. FINISHING RESIN (NON-AIR INHIBITED, CONTAINS WAX)

Of course, there are many other types of polyester resins which may be available, such as "casting resin" or "tank resin". But laminating and finishing resins are the types most applicable to sheathing work and the novice should stick to these. There are some manufacturers who formulate variations on these two resin types and give them other names, such as "sanding resin" or "surfacing resin", but these still fall into the two categories. They either contain wax or they don't.

ORTHO, ISO, & VINYLESTER RESINS

"Ortho", "iso", and "vinylester" are variations and modifications made to the basic types of polyester resins with regard to their chemical molecular basis. Ortho resins (technically called "orthophthalic resins") and iso resins (technically called "isophthalic resins") refer to differences in the acid base of the resin. The ortho resins are less complex from a molecular standpoint than iso resins, while the vinylester types are more complex molecularly than either the iso or ortho types. However, they are ALL polyester types, although the vinylesters are known as "modified" polyesters, and some call them a cross between polyester and epoxy resins.

While this last paragraph may seem confusing, to keep things simple, ortho resin is the most common variety of polyester resin and will suffice for the majority of sheathing applications when a polyester resin is selected. Why? Primarily due to lower cost, and because the qualities offered by either the iso or vinylester varieties are usually not needed, although the use of iso resins is on the increase.

Why pick one over another? Both iso and vinylester resins have higher physical properties than ortho resins and impart improved characteristics to a laminate. For example, iso resins have better corrosion and solvent resistance than ortho resins, and are also somewhat tougher with better impact strength. Thus iso resins have an advantage over ortho resins at least in theory. But in thin film coatings such as those applicable to sheathing work, experience shows little difference in performance to justify the added cost, although iso resins are entirely suitable.

The picture changes with vinylester resins, however. While these are even better than iso or ortho resins with regard to chemical and corrosion resistance, both ortho and iso resin are entirely adequate for marine use in this regard. Vinylester resins also retain high strength properties at higher temperatures, and while this quality has made vinylester popular for storage tank fabrication, aerospace, and other industrial applications, boats are not subjected to high temperatures in normal use.

Vinylester resins also have an inherent elongation flexibility that gives laminates made from this resin an improvement where certain high stresses cannot be eliminated in the design process, such as mechanical cycling and vibration. However, epoxy resins (to be described) are also excellent in this regard, and incorporate several other additional advantages over vinylesters.

A problem with vinylester resins is that many are more complicated to use, especially for the novice. Shelf life is frequently much less than regular polyester resins. Thus many are sold as unpromoted resins requiring the ultimate user to add the promotor. Further complicating this is the fact that different and more complex promotor systems are often used. For example, some products require not only the addition of cobalt, but also dimethylanaline (or "DMA"), an extremely dangerous product and a carcinogen.

Because two promotors may be required as well as the addition of the M-E-K peroxide catalyst, vinylester resins can be more difficult to work with regarding gel times and curing procedures because of the varying proportions of the three ingredients. This can be tricky for the amateur and lead to questionable results. Because of these problems, some experts recommend the use of vinylester resins only by experienced or industrial users. Because of the variety of curing systems available, if one intends to use vinylester resins, he should contact the resin supplier for advice. However, for the majority of sheathing applications, the additional cost and trouble of vinylesters isn't worth it; epoxy resins are more suitable if one feels that polyesters are not good enough.

GEL COAT

Gel coat is a form of polyester resin (either ortho or iso based) often discussed. A gel coat is simply a layer of pigmented resin ordinarily applied to the female mold surface in the production of fiberglass boats built using this process. The gel coat resin is usually sprayed onto the mold surface and allowed to set or "gel" before applying the first layer of fiberglass material in the lay-up laminating process. This definition is somewhat over-simplified because gel coats are a special field in themselves and require different formulations and characteristics than ordinary laminating or finishing resins.

Since gel coats are air inhibited (wax-free), gel coat resins are rarely used in sheathing work where the gel coat would be the final coating. While a wax solution can be added, or a PVA release agent can be sprayed over the gel coat surface, or parting film can be applied over the gel coat to make it cure, these methods are usually only suitable over small areas such as would occur in repair work.

Gel coat manufacturers prefer spray application and do NOT recommend applying gel coats with a brush. Some of the reasons include the following. Like all polyester resins, gel coat does not apply like a paint. It is difficult to flow on and level out with a brush. For this reason, the uniform thickness necessary for a good gel coat application is virtually impossible to maintain and verify. This leads to surface flaws and ap-

plication problems which may be impossible to correct. In general, the success of a good gel coat is dependent on how quickly, evenly, and thoroughly it can be applied.

In view of the foregoing, and since it is impractical to work more than a small area with a brush at a time, successful results are seldom achieved by using a brush. Finally, the glossy luster of the gel coated surface resulting from the female mold surface does not exist in a sheathing situation. When gel coat is applied as a final OUTSIDE coating, unless the entire gel coated surface is leveled out with a Mylar covering (a tricky operation best left to professionals if done at all!), an acceptable surface will not result; sanding and finishing will still be required. For proper appearance and durability, a paint or coating system would still be recommended since gel coats are not durable over the long term.

While this elaboration on gel coats may seem unnecessary, since they have little place in sheathing work, sooner or later the question invariably comes up as to why it is not recommended that gel coats be used EXCEPT for the purpose for which they were intended. This purpose is for spray application in female mold fiberglass boatbuilding, and the preceding points out the problems if this purpose is deviated from. If one insists on working with gel coats, contact one of the gel coat manufacturers directly and discuss your situation with them for whatever recommendations they may have.

EPOXY RESINS

Epoxies are a whole separate division of industrial chemicals that are more complicated and complex than polyesters. They come in a huge variety of products and systems in a wide array of viscosities ranging from super penetrating fluids thinner than water to nearly inflexible clay-like putties and fillers. Generally the firms involved in manufacturing epoxies are not involved in making polyester resins (at least not in the same plants), and vice versa; that's how different the chemical and manufacturing processes are.

This wide array of epoxy products can be confusing to the consumer and makes it difficult to select a product suitable for the application of a sheathing material. Part of the problem is that epoxies are two-part materials consisting of an epoxy resin (or part "A" as it is known in the trade), and a curing agent or "hardener" (or part "B" as it is called). This is unlike polyester resins whose curing agent consists of a very small amount of one kind of catalyst to set up the internally generated heat, and which has no bearing on the characteristics of the resin or its viscosity.

With epoxy products, BOTH the qualities of the resin AND the hardener must be considered in how the product will handle and perform. This is because the hardeners make up a high percentage of the mix. For example, typical proportions of resin to hardener include 1:1, 2:1, 3:1, 4:1, and 5:1 ratios. These ratios are the result of the many possible combinations of epoxy categories and the characteristics that are desired in each, but otherwise have little or no bearing on the consumer as such. To make matters more confusing, a certain epoxy resin may be used with a wide array of hardener types, AND even in varying proportions, depending on the results desired (however, always use the products per the instructions in any case).

Unlike polyester resins, all epoxies are tenacious bonding agents or "glues", and generally have excellent shock absorption qualities. Some are formulated just for gluing purposes and are not intended for sheathing applications where wetting out a reinforcing material is required. Other formulations are super-thin penetrating fluid products which are too thin to build up coats of the thickness necessary in sheathing applications. Still other products are

putty-like substances meant only for use as fillers.

Then too, some products are meant for coating purposes, and while they may appear to be of suitable viscosity for applying a sheathing of fiberglass, they may not wet out the sheathing material properly. Thus the novice must depend to a large extent on what the product label or manufacturer says a particular epoxy product (or "system" as it is called) is for. For sheathings using fiberglass and similar materials, an epoxy that is intended for laminating purposes should always be used.

In general, epoxies are tougher, stronger, and more flexible than polyesters, and highly impermeable to water, making them well suited for sealing, sheathing, and coating purposes, especially on wood surfaces. In fact, epoxy resin products have been formulated and developed into what are best described as "encapsulation systems" that have advanced the state of amateur wood boatbuilding remarkably in recent years (see Chapter 9).

EPOXY SAFETY

In general, epoxy resins require greater care in use than polyesters. Just about all epoxy systems can cause dermatitis, skin burns, and respiratory problems if proper precautions are not taken. The problem with many beginners is that they don't realize that the toxic effects of epoxies are cumulative; over time, if precautions are not taken to protect the skin and respiratory system, the body will absorb the materials with no apparent reaction until a certain threshold is reached (which varies in each person).

Once this threshold is exceeded, a sudden and often severe, reaction can occur, usually in the form of a poison ivy-like skin rash in any part of the body; not necessarily where contact was made. In super-sensitive people, hospitalization may be required.

22

Once this sensitization has occurred, the person must stop using the product, and often must avoid being around it at all. In severe cases, symptoms can recur even at a much later date if the person attempts to use the products again. In such cases, the person must simply avoid the products entirely. Thus, the following safety precautions apply particularly to the use of epoxy products:

AVOID DIRECT SKIN OR EYE CONTACT. ALWAYS WEAR SKIN PROTECTION OF THE PROPER TYPE. AVOID INHALATION OF VAPORS OR SANDING DUST. ALWAYS WORK IN WELL VENTILATED CONDITIONS. WHEN SANDING EPOXY COATED SURFACES, ALWAYS WEAR A SUITABLE DUST MASK. WHEN POURING AND MIXING THE PRODUCTS, WEAR EYE PROTECTION. KEEP THE PRODUCTS AWAY FROM CHILDREN OR ANIMALS. FOR MORE INFORMATION, READ CHAPTER 5, "SAFETY".

WHY USE EPOXIES?

While polyesters have occupied a majority of the market in resins for boat work over the years, there are certain aspects of epoxies which make them superior to polyesters, and as a result, the use of epoxies is on the increase. In some sheathing applications ONLY epoxies are suitable.

As noted, epoxy resins have superior bonding strength. Also, in general, epoxy coatings virtually do not shrink, and exhibit some degree of flexibility. Thus epoxy coatings tend not to be brittle, and this quality, along with minimal shrinkage, prevents or minimizes surface cracking. Water vapor transmission is also superior to polyesters; epoxy coatings keep water out which protects wood substrates from rot, water absorption, and weathering better than do polyesters. It is this quality which has al-

lowed the development of so-called "wood-epoxy encapsulation systems".

In sheathing applications over the following materials, epoxy systems are highly recommended, or a "must". These include aluminum, steel, teak, oak, redwood, western red cedar, cypress, concrete (e.g. ferro-cement), as well as other non-porous materials. This is because of the superior bonding strength of epoxies. However, proper surface preparation is critical to a durable, long-lived application over such difficult-to-bond-to materials, and some of these techniques are given in Chapter 8.

The qualities of high bonding strength, flexibility, and absence of shrinkage give epoxy coated surfaces higher fatigue resistance than polyester coated surfaces. In high-cycle testing, polyester laminate samples showed a somewhat higher one-time load-to-failure strength over a comparable epoxy sample, but polyester laminates retained less than ⅕ of their original strength. On the other hand, epoxy samples retained a greater percentage of their original static strength after high-cycle testing, but withstood considerably more cycles. Since repeated stresses are normal on a boat, this is one reason why epoxy resins are more durable than polyesters.

The primary disadvantage of epoxy systems is cost, which is usually considerably more than polyesters, while minor disadvantages involve safety and handling problems discussed, which are somewhat more critical than with polyesters. In addition, a suitable epoxy system must be used for sheathing applications if application and curing problems are to be avoided.

Thus the user must determine what his requirements and expectations will be as they relate to the boat in question. Is the boat worth the extra expense of epoxies? Will the boat be kept long enough to warrant the cost? Does the user want to subject himself to the added problems associated with epoxies? Since application methods are basically the same for both polyester and epoxy resins, the decision to sheathe with one or the other resins should be based primarily on the answers to these questions.

POLYESTER & EPOXY CONDITIONS OF USE

Both polyester and epoxy resins are affected by ambient temperatures and conditions, such as humidity and sunlight. Cold temperatures slow down the cure and may even prevent it, while warm temperatures speed it up; if it's too hot, there may not be sufficient time to work the resin.

Recommended working temperatures should be between 70°F to 85°F for polyester resin. Normal epoxy resin laminating systems are also suitable within this range, although some products are available with special hardeners that allow somewhat more temperature latitude, either higher or lower. While it's possible to work in temperatures higher than 85°F with either epoxy or polyester resin, you'll have to work much faster and/or work smaller sections at a time, although temperatures approaching 100°F become impractical in most cases.

For colder climates, it is possible to obtain so-called "cold weather" polyesters which allow temperatures in use down to about 60°F. Such "cold weather" resins usually include a higher percentage of cobalt promoter, and sometimes this can be added to the resin by the user for the same effect. Check with your resin supplier if this is recommended. Generally, NEVER do fiberglassing with polyester resins below 60°F. There is a danger that your laminate will absorb moisture, not cure, and lose physical characteristics. While it is possible to add more catalyst and speed up the reaction of polyester resins, this is not usually advisable since it can affect physical characteristics and increase shrinkage.

With epoxy resins, do NOT attempt to speed up the cure by adding more hardener or vary the resin-to-hardener ratio from that recommended on the label. Epoxy resins are systems that are formulated to have certain properties and characteristics within certain temperature ranges resulting from the resin/hardener combination in just the proportions stated on the product labels. Varying these can lead to problems and questionable results.

The curing time or the "exothermic reaction" of both epoxy and polyester resins can be varied in several ways from the normal pot life listed for any given product. Resin tends to set up quicker in large, concentrated masses rather than in smaller amounts or when dispersed over a large area or shallow container. Thus, to increase the pot life, mix smaller batches, or pour the mix into shallow pans such as paint trays. The mixed resin can also be kept on ice or in a cooler, or in the shade, or even in a refrigerator as long as foodstuffs are protected. Then too, unmixed products can be stored before use at lower temperatures (below 70°, but not freezing), and this is recommended in warm climates.

However, while little viscosity change is noticeable in polyesters within normal ranges, such is not the case with epoxies. These become more viscous at lower temperatures, making them more difficult to mix and use, even though the product may eventually set up.

In cooler weather, to speed up the cure, mix up larger batches and let them set a while before using; this will give the reaction some time to begin before application. Also, warm up the products somewhat before mixing, such as setting the containers in warm water. Similarly, the surfaces on which the products will be applied should also be up to normal ranges. A couple of critically placed heat lamps, light bulbs, or use of a hot air gun can help in this regard. However, do NOT use open flames for this purpose, and be sure that any such heat-producing appliance will not cause damage to the surface.

Humidity and sunlight have an effect on the resin also. Humid conditions can affect the cure time and inhibit the cure as well as affect surface quality, and lead to cloudy coatings with many epoxies. Likewise, direct sunlight can disturb the sanding qualities of the resin, speed up the cure, affect surface quality, and cause shrinkage in polyester laminates. For these reasons, work should always be done indoors or at least in areas protected from the direct effects of sunlight and humidity. If work must take place outdoors, a temporary structure should be made to protect the work area.

Finally, NEVER thin polyester or epoxy resins for sheathing work. While thinning may be done in certain applications with certain products, the thinners do have an adverse affect on the resin which can lead to numerous problems. For example, volatile solvents such as acetone can be entrapped in the resin, causing a reduction in physical properties, increased water permeability, and possible cure failure.

STORAGE & SHELF LIFE

The shelf life of both polyester and epoxy products can vary depending on the product as well as how it was handled from manufacture to retailer. Ordinarily, polyesters will be usable for at least six months from date of purchase, and often up to a year or so. However, if the resin is NOT used within six months, it should be stored in a cool place out of direct sunlight at temperatures NOT OVER 75°F, but above freezing (above 60° is preferable).

Epoxies generally have a longer shelf life; two years is not unusual, although the shelf life of both the resin and hardener must be considered and each may vary. Epoxies subjected to freezing or other unusual storage conditions may develop hard, crystal-like substances, particularly in the bottom

of the container. These can be dissolved by setting the container in warm water for a period of time; after the crystals disappear, the product can be used.

Always keep containers sealed when not in use to keep volatile constituents from evaporating and reducing the potency of the products. Also, certain products (especially epoxies) can absorb moisture vapor in high humidity conditions if the containers are left open. If the epoxy stands for a long period of time, stir or agitate each ingredient before use. Ingredients should never be exposed to extremes of heat or cold, or freezing/thawing cycles. If in doubt about a product's performance due to long storage, mix up a small batch; if it sets up in approximately the time stipulated, it should be satisfactory. With polyesters, if the viscosity seems thick or lumpy or gelatinous, do NOT use it.

THIXOTROPY

Many think that a thixotropic resin is one that is "thick". Others think that a thixotropic resin is one that won't run or sag. These are both misconceptions. The term "thixotropic" defines the quality of a resin to thicken at rest, but become fluid again on agitation and stirring. In practical respects, the tendency for a resin to run or sag in use is MINIMIZED by the quality of thixotropy.

Thixotropy should not be confused with the term, viscosity, or the ability of a resin to resist flow. Viscosity is the result of the chemical manufacturing process, while thixotropic qualities usually are provided by the addition of thixotropic agents or fillers AFTER the resin is made, and may also contribute to the resin's viscosity. Methods will be explained in Chapter 9 on how to increase the thixotropic quality of a resin.

However, the main reason for discussing this subject is the misconception that there are resins that won't run or sag, a potential problem on vertical surfaces that frightens some amateurs. The fact is that any resin worth using for a sheathing application, be it polyester or epoxy, will run or sag on inclined or vertical surfaces IF TOO MUCH IS APPLIED. While a resin could conceivably be made that would NOT run or sag, it also would NOT wet out the material, at least before curing would occur, and it would probably be brittle and shrink. Thus while some resin may be more or less thixotropic than others, this quality is not critical if proper application practices are followed. Beware of resins which emphasize this quality over all others.

CHAPTER 5   Safety

When working with fiberglass materials and resins, safety CANNOT be over-stressed. The four most important categories of safety (not necessarily in any order of importance) when doing work with fiberglass materials and resins are:

1. FIRE SAFETY
2. EYE HAZARDS
3. BODILY CONTACT WITH TOXIC SUBSTANCES
4. INHALATION OF TOXIC ELEMENTS

In addition to the above, do NOT ingest any of the products; this can be fatal, particularly in the case of catalyst used with polyester resin. If ingestion occurs, call a physician or get emergency help immediately. If catalyst is swallowed, take large quantities of water or milk.

Instead of writing a verbose, boring chapter on safety which many might choose to ignore, the following is a list of various things to do and not to do so that the reader can quickly refer to this section before the work begins. This method should make the references more handy to use. In any case, anyone planning to use fiberglass and resin should know and understand the following safety precautions PRIOR to doing any work or using the materials.

1. Do NOT smoke while working with fiberglass and resin, or any flammable solvents. Avoid all open flames in the working area, especially pilot lights on appliances, as well as other sources of heat that could ignite a fire.

2. ALWAYS work in a well-ventilated area. If necessary, set up some slow speed fans to insure a complete movement of air. However, avoid high speed fans that might remove volatiles too rapidly and affect cure, or that could blow dust and other debris onto a wet laminate.

3. Avoid prolonged breathing of fumes from resins, hardeners, cobalt promotors, catalysts, styrene, and solvents. Read the hazard labels on all products regarding exposure prior to using them and note what steps to take in the event of excessive exposure.

4. Wear a respirator or protective breathing mask when sanding, spray painting, spraying polyester resin, or when mixing or sanding filler materials such as microspheres or thixotropic additives.

5. Wear eye-protective gear such as glasses, goggles, or a face mask, especially when mixing resins with catalysts or hardeners. If any of these materials get into your eyes, flood with copious amounts of water. Seek emergency help immediately, explaining to those administering aid what the products involved in the accident were.

6. If epoxy resins or hardeners come into contact with the skin, WASH IMMEDIATELY with soap and water. This solution works better with a small percentage of household ammonia added.

For polyester resins OR epoxy resins, special resin cleaning products are made for this purpose which are even better, and are recommended. Rub off excess resin first prior to application of such products.

7. Do NOT mix cobalt accelerator directly with MEK peroxide catalyst as a violent reaction and/or explosion will occur. Also, do not mix MEK peroxide catalyst with acetone.

8. Do NOT use ketone-based or chlorinated solvents to remove resins or hardeners from the skin. These products (e.g. acetone, lacquer thinner, etc.) open the pores and drive the products further into the skin, and may cause skin irritation themselves. NEVER use solvents contaminated with resin on the skin.

9. ALWAYS wear skin protection, including barrier creams as a minimum on exposed skin, and gloves. While inexpensive disposable vinyl gloves are acceptable with polyester resins, butyl rubber gloves are considered best for epoxy resins and hardeners. Do NOT reuse used disposable gloves. For added comfort and to minimize sweating, use thin white cotton inner liners under such gloves or use lined gloves. Disposable paper aprons will help keep resin off clothing. Resin spilled on clothing should be removed to avoid skin contact.

10. Do NOT try home remedies if toxic symptoms or extreme dermatitis develops. See a physician and explain what chemicals you have been working with.

11. ALWAYS read instructions carefully and follow them to the letter on all products you may be using.

12. Dispose of gelled resin properly by first dispersing it well over a broad area, preferably the ground, for later placing in proper containers once cured. Concentrated batches of resin which have begun to cure can get hot enough to smoke and ignite adjacent combustible materials. Do NOT dump such resin into trash barrels containing refuse.

13. Keep children, pets, and other people NOT familiar with the hazards of the products out of the work area.

14. Keep a FIRST AID kit handy as well as a CLASS "B" fire extinguisher, and have access to a telephone. Try not to work alone or be remote from assistance if you need it.

15. Keep your work area tidy and clean. Do NOT allow sanding dust or sawdust to accumulate; these are hazardous to breathe and can be combustible in the proper concentrations.

16. Scoop up spilled resin, or absorb it with an inert material, such as sand or vermiculite, and dispose of it into a closed non-combustible container. Wash the contaminated area with trisodium phosphate and water.

17. MEK peroxide is an "organic peroxide" that will oxidize and corrode many metals, including steel, brass, copper, and aluminum. Thus it is classed as a "hazardous material" that is illegal to ship on an airplane.

18. Do NOT expose catalyst to any form of heat, sunlight, or elevated temperatures.

If you DO take care with resin products and related materials, treat them with the respect they deserve, and follow all the above safety practices, you will have few problems or hazards to contend with.

CHAPTER 6   How Much Will You Need?

The amount of fiberglass and resin materials needed to do a given job will vary depending on the area to be covered, the sizes of fiberglass materials available, and the composition of the fiberglass materials used (e.g. cloth, mat, or woven roving). Also, the manner in which the material is applied to the surface (e.g. lengthwise or crosswise) will have a bearing on the amount of material necessary, considering overlaps, corners, etc.

Another consideration may be how far one is from a source. Generally speaking, it is best to buy too much rather than not enough material, as it always seems that more material is required than planned, and you don't want to run short at a critical time, especially if your supplier is some distance away. Of course, mistakes can happen, so it's best to figure a little extra just for such eventualities.

FIGURING RESIN

The amount of resin required depends on the type of fiberglass material being used and, to some extent, on the viscosity of the resin. Figuring the amount of resin if working on cloth is much easier than for mat and woven roving. Polyester, and epoxy resins of similar viscosity, will saturate approximately the same amount of fiberglass cloth.

If using 10-ounce fiberglass cloth, one gallon of resin will provide three coats of resin (the normal number of coatings in such an application) for approximately each 40 to 45 square feet of area. If using 7½-

ounce fiberglass cloth, one gallon can cover an area between 50 and 60 square feet using three coats. Still lighter cloth would allow commensurately more coverage per gallon.

When figuring coverage for epoxy resin, the above figures include both the resin and hardener combined. However, in many cases, epoxy products are sold by weight, NOT per gallon or fluid measure. Also, some epoxy systems have ratios that do not equate to gallons precisely, so you may need to interpret what is available to the amount of coverage possible. If in doubt, your supplier should be able to help you.

Getting an exact estimate of polyester resin if using mat or woven roving is difficult because of the varying weights of material. Also, some materials tend to wet out better and faster with less resin than others. One way to determine the amount of resin with mat and woven roving is to use the method that fiberglass boat manufacturers and naval architects use; glass/resin ratios. For example, a typical mat laminate should contain about 30% fiberglass material and about 70% resin by weight. A woven roving laminate should contain about 45% fiberglass material and 55% resin content. A variation of 5% plus or minus is usually acceptable. If mat and woven roving are combined, figure ⅓ to ⅔ resin.

Because it's difficult to go to a supplier and actually weigh the materials, the following examples should be of help. If using 2-ounce (per square foot) mat, using the 30%/70% glass/resin ratio noted above for mat, one gallon of typical polyester resin weighing approximately 9 lbs. per gallon (or about 145 ounces) will saturate an area of about 30 square feet (2 oz. × 30 sq. ft. = 60 oz. of fiberglass which is 30% of the layup) + 140 oz. of resin will be required (or one gallon, which is approximately the

additional 70% portion).

If using 24-ounce (per square yard) woven roving with the noted 45%/55% glass/resin ratio, one gallon of resin will saturate approximately 45 square feet (or 5

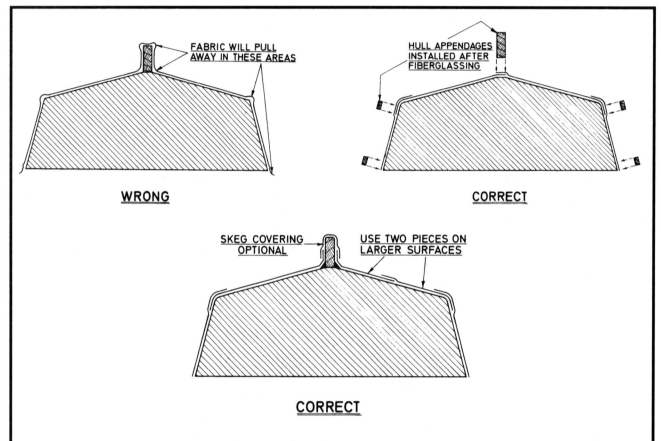

HOW TO UTILIZE SHEATHING FABRICS

In sheathing a boat with cloth, success of the job depends partly on how the material is used. While a simple small boat may be covered with a single layer of cloth, a boat of larger size or with varying contours and angles is best covered in several pieces or "panels" which will allow the material to conform to the surfaces better.

For example, in the illustrations, the hull section to the upper left has been covered from sheer to sheer in one piece of cloth, even over the protruding skeg. Several things are wrong with such a practice. In the example, no corners have been radiused which means that the cloth will pull away from these areas. Even if the corners were radiused, there would be a problem keeping the cloth in position in one area while another area was being worked. Even on a small boat, it would be very difficult to work an area with this many surface direction changes before the resin set up. In short, the job would probably turn out a mess.

The other examples (above right and center) show the correct manner in utilizing the cloth. Whenever possible, all hull append-

ages should be removed and the cloth then applied after proper surface preparation. If an appendage (such as the skeg in the center example) cannot be removed, then at least the inside corners should be filleted or fitted with cant strips. In this case, the bottom panels lap only partially onto the skeg each side, and a small piece of cloth is used to cap the skeg.

Where the boat is fairly large, it is often better to do the bottom in two panels per side. The reason is much the same as in the first example. There will be a tendency for the material to pull away from the skeg as the material is worked closer to the chine edge. It can also be difficult to work such a large area fast enough.

The example above right will prove the easiest to apply because the appendages have been removed thereby reducing the number of surfaces to be covered at one time. After the application, the appendages are reinstalled. These can be bedded in resin saturated scraps of cloth or mat for bonding in place. Or if they are to be removable in the future, they are best bedded in a non-hardening marine-type mastic.

30

square yards × 24 oz. = 120 oz. of fiber-glass which is 45% of the layup) + 146 oz. of resin will be required (or about one gallon, which is the additional 55% of the layup). If mat and woven roving are combined in a laminate, for each pound or unit of weight of fiberglass used, figure two pounds or units of weight of resin for a ⅓-to-⅔ glass/resin ratio.

Of course, the above figures are ideal and don't take into account any material which will be wasted or any problems associated with saturating the material. If anything, these figures are somewhat optimistic based on experience, and they do assume an ideal resin/glass ratio which may be difficult to achieve and maintain. While only a few examples are given, it would not take much effort to project from these figures to suit varying material weights. If the fiberglass material being used is somewhat lighter or heavier, just vary the resin portion proportionately.

In figuring the amount of catalyst required for polyester resins, note that most resin manufacturers provide pre-measured containers in the correct amount per each quantity of resin purchased. Sometimes more might be required, however, depending on ambient temperatures, so it may be advisable to order an extra container or two of catalyst just in case, but not more than 25% more than that provided with the original quantity of resin.

FIGURING FIBERGLASS MATERIALS

Fiberglass materials, whether cloth, mat, woven roving, or other combinations, are usually sold by the running yard, although in bulk quantities, they may be available by the roll for cloth and by weight in mat or woven roving if one is willing to purchase an entire roll. Widths for all these materials will commonly be 38", 44", 50", or 60", however, not all these sizes may be in stock for all items from any given supplier.

As noted before, coverage depends on the direction the material is applied, the number and size of expected overlaps (if any), and the widths of material available or that will be used (which will partly determine the number of overlaps and joints necessary).

In general, it is usually easiest to lay the material lengthwise along a boat hull, deck, or cabin top. However, there are exceptions where it might be easier to set the material transversely or even diagonally. An instance where this might be the case would be on round-bilged, deep-keeled sailboats. In any case, the job will probably be easier if the materials are utilized so as to keep the number of joints and laps to a minimum. And because there will be more laps if working transversely, it is generally easier to do the job using a lengthwise orientation (see Chapter 9 for more information concerning joints and laps).

In sheathing work using fiberglass cloth, joints between widths of cloth should be overlapped. Butt joints, especially in single layers of cloth are not recommended. However, with epoxy resin, since it does not shrink as much and has better bond strength, such laps are often optional.

With polyester resin using heavier materials such as mat and woven roving, for example, butt joints are more practical and easily made. With cloth, mat, or woven roving, butt joints should be used wherever two or more layers of these materials will be used, with such butt joints staggered a good distance away from any adjacent butt joints. So in figuring the amount of fiberglass cloth required, determine extra material for any laps if and where required.

As noted, for hull covering work, the way the material is used will vary with the hull form as well as to suit the widths of materials available. For example, on some small round-bilge hulls, it may be possible to cover the entire hull in a single width of cloth running lengthwise without joints. On larger round-bilge hulls, an overlap joint can be made along the centerline at the keel and a single width used along the half girth of the hull running lengthwise each side up to the sheer rails.

With small hard-chine hulls, it may be possible to also get by with a single width of cloth for the bottom, overlapping along the keel centerline and over the chine onto the sides several inches. Then use one width of cloth for each side which will overlap onto the bottom another several inches at the chines. This forms a double layer of material at the chine junction, an area that often takes a lot of abuse, thus providing desirable extra protection.

Ordinarily, figure the length required by actually measuring along the hull in one direction only. Do not try to measure the cloth and figure what the exact shape of the cloth will be in the hopes of saving material. In other words, place a tape measure along the keel or sheer, for example, and buy material in this length in at least the maximum width needed to cover the area PLUS allowances for overlaps along the length of the cloth if required. Keep in mind that wide widths of cloth can be cut lengthwise to make any number of smaller widths that may be required.

In many cases, especially on longer boats, joints in the cloth are considered a normal occurrence since the supplier may not always provide exact lengths of cloth in single pieces to cover a given area. Thus in measuring, allow an extra foot or so for such overlaps, as well as additional material for the overlaps at each end. If the boat has a transom stern, or an actual appendage keel (as opposed to simply a skeg), figure enough material for these areas as well. Be sure to allow enough material for DOUBLE LAPS when using cloth and polyester resins along the chines, keel, stem, transom corners, etc., except on the very smallest, simple boats where lapped corners may not be necessary. Such laps may be optional with epoxy resins (see Chapter 9).

HOW THICK?

There is a tendency among amateur boatbuilders and those wanting to do fiberglass sheathing applications to "overbuild", or add more material in the hopes of gaining more strength, etc. While extra material may be desirable in some cases at some areas (e.g. extra reinforcing along chine junctions on plywood boats), remember that fiberglass coverings are not as stiff as wood or plywood, nor as strong on a weight basis. Thus, indiscriminate additions of sheathing materials may accomplish little or nothing in terms of adding stiffness, and if extra strength was desired in the boatbuilding project, an increase in planking thickness would probably do more at less increase in weight.

As the chart at the end of this chapter shows, weight will be increased by adding material, and performance could be impaired if too much weight is added. Of course, more materials mean more cost and work. So the best advice is to stick to the designer's recommendations if building a boat, and for recovering of existing boats, it's best to keep sheathing layers as thin as possible commensurate with the durability and protection desired.

The chart gives some idea how thick the various materials will be when applied over a surface. For materials which are heavier or lighter in weight, extrapolate from the figures given to arrive at an approximate figure. While weight per square foot figures are given per layer for several types of materials, and the weights of additional layers can be projected from these figures, note that additional layers will, in practice, weigh somewhat less per layer than the initial layer since bonding coats are not required, etc. However, the figures listed will give estimations that are close enough in most cases.

FIBERGLASS THICKNESS WITH RESIN

Weight per layer (Lbs.) per Sq. Ft. (Approx.)

Number of layers		1	2	3	4	5	6	7
2 oz. mat	.413	.058″	.116″	.175″	.237″	.299″	.361″	.423″
24 oz. woven roving	.334	.036″	.071″	.109″	.147″	.185″	.223″	.262″
10 oz. cloth	.14	.016″	.032″	.048″	.064″	.080″	.095″	.111″

Variations of plus or minus 10 percent may occur with mat, somewhat less with woven roving and cloth.

NOTE: To convert the above figures to ordinary fractions or metric approximations:

1/64″ = .016″ or .4 mm
1/32″ = .031″ or .8 mm
1/16″ = .063″ or 1.6 mm
1/8″ = .125″ or 3.2 mm
1/4″ = .25″ or 6.4 mm

CHAPTER 7

Tools & Equipment

The tools and equipment required will vary depending on the size of the boat being worked on, as well as the complexity of the job at hand. If simply sheathing the exterior of a new small plywood hull, for example, not as many tools or as much equipment and supplies would be required as if recovering a large existing hull which might require considerable surface preparation in addition to certain hull modifications for a suitable fiberglass application.

Because of possible variations such as the above, specific tools cannot be recommended for all jobs. Instead, tools and equipment will be discussed in some detail and then the reader can decide what will be required for his particular application. After reading what follows, it will be easier to determine the tools and equipment, as well as the amount of supplies, that will be necessary to do a particular job. The list at the end of this chapter can be used as a guide in preparing for the job and checking to see that all tools, equipment, and supplies will be provided and ready to use.

SANDERS & SANDPAPER

If you're the he-man type or a brute for punishment, it is conceivable that any areas could be hand sanded as required, especially if the job being done is small or not of much consequence. But even when working on a small boat, a lot of blood, sweat, and tears will be saved by using power sanders. And because the boat can't be taken to the equipment in most cases, the hand portable type tools (either electric

or pneumatic powered) are recommended.

Three types of sanders are generally available; these being belt sanders, disc sanders, and finish sanders with either reciprocating action, orbital action, or both. If you don't have these machines, they can often be rented, or you might borrow them from a friend who may not be aware of the punishment you are about to deliver onto his tools.

In any case, get the most rugged, heavy-duty equipment available because using sanders in fiberglass work is a severe test of any power tool. The cheap lightweight equipment commonly being sold at discount stores just does not stand up to the arduous continuous-duty use required in fiberglassing. While price is not always a method to measure quality, a seemingly expensive sander suited to commercial duty will usually outlast several low quality "price" sanders, making apparently expensive equipment cheaper in the long run.

Depending on the job being done, all three types of sanders may be required. In fact, you'll work a lot less if you have all three types even though it may be possible to get by with less. If you must narrow the choice to one type of sander, a disc sander will probably be the most versatile. A disc sander is perfect for feathering edges of fiberglass material, grinding down unfair surfaces, trimming hardened edges, and general fairing purposes. However, a disc sander does take some practice to master. It's easy to gouge the surface or remove too much material. Thus to prevent this tendency, get some practice, and also make use of one of the foam pad backing disc attachments commonly available.

Belt sanders are ideal for removing old paint during surface preparation. Belt sanders can also be used to smooth out uneven surfaces, and some prefer them for fairing surfaces (at least in flatter areas). They also remove a lot of material rapidly, and as with a disc sander, a little practice is required to keep from gouging the surface. In this regard, a heavier machine that doesn't tend to skip around is preferable to lighter weight equipment.

When using such a machine, hold the sander without bearing down too much on the surface; this allows the belt to do the work without gouging the surface. A more even surface results if you work the machine back and forth instead of from side to side, being careful to keep the sanding surface as level as possible.

Finish sanders don't remove much material, and for this reason, they can be used with a heavy hand on fiberglass work without fear of damaging the surface. This feature makes their use quite suitable for the inexperienced, but conversely, they are slow and tedious. However, for final finish work, they are almost a necessity, especially if large areas are involved.

Although most good quality sanders have dust bag attachments, there will still be a lot of dust flying about, and much of this dust will be filled with fine glass particles. These glass particles can cause premature wear of the brushes, and sometimes the bearings in some tool motors, especially those of lower quality.

When sanding, because of the dust in the air, a protective mask should be considered mandatory. Inexpensive disposable types

These are the three types of sanders used for sheathing work as described in the text. Commercial duty tools are preferable.

are suitable for this purpose as are the type with replaceable elements. In addition, protective body clothing and head gear (a paper sack with a rubber band works well to keep dust out of your hair) will prevent or minimize the itching, irritation, and mess caused by the glass dust.

If working with epoxy resins, such protection is even more important. Ordinarily sanding can take place on epoxy coated surfaces once the resin is hard, but it still may not be totally cured (it takes several days or more for this to happen with most epoxies). Thus, in addition to any ground glass, such sanding dust can be considered hazardous, both from skin contact and inhalation. Sensitization to epoxies can result if proper protection is not used.

Even though power sanders can be extensively used in just about any project, most jobs will still require some amount of hand sanding. This is especially true around inside and outside corners where power equipment will easily grind away too much material, or in areas too small or confined for the tools where it may actually be easier to hand sand. Thus a good sanding block comes in handy; you can buy these or make your own from any suitably sized block of wood.

For fiberglass work, use commercial duty sandpaper such as aluminum oxide, silicon carbide, or comparable types. Ordinary flint paper (the vanilla colored stuff often sold in grocery stores) or the reddish garnet paper commonly used in woodworking will wear out quickly in fiberglass work; these papers are a waste of money.

While the better sandpaper types are more expensive initially, they hold their grit much longer, and do not load up as quickly, especially when the recommended "open coat" type is used (try cleaning sanding discs with acetone for longer life). Thus they are worth the added initial cost.

The question of what degree of grit (coarseness or fineness) of sandpaper to buy and how much will depend on the size of job and the quality of finish that's desired or acceptable. In buying sandpaper, there's a number on the back of the paper telling the degree of coarseness (or fineness) of the paper. The larger the number, the finer the grit of the sandpaper. For example, a #24 paper is quite coarse, while a #600 paper is very fine and intended for final finish work. Such fine paper is usually classed as a "wet-or-dry" type; that is, it can be used with water to make exceptionally smooth, fine, clear, and glossy surfaces. Comparable grit papers are available in disc form also for use with disc sanders. The tacky pressure-sensitive type are simple and effective.

For a disc or belt sander, probably one or two coarse grit papers somewhere between a #25 and #50 grit will suffice for all but finish work. In any case, don't be afraid of buying too much sandpaper as it can always be used in the future, especially if you are a boat owner or hobbyist.

SHAPING TOOLS

Depending on the job, some tools may be required for shaping not only wood members to be fiberglassed, but also various shaped, curved, or filleted areas made from various fillers or putties. For woodwork, these can include wood rasps, woodworking files, and wood planes. In addition, for woodwork as well as for use on many filler materials, one of the most versatile tool types are the various patented surface-forming tools under the "Surform" designation.

An ordinary putty knife will be required for working with putty and filler. Shaping fillets can be done with the edge of a suitably radiused, plastic lid, or radiused piece of wood, or even the back of a spoon. In fact, the number and type of such shaping tools is limited only by the worker's imagination. In any case, such tools should be ready when needed if required for the work.

APPLICATION TOOLS

Tools used for applying fiberglass materials consist mainly of brushes, rollers, and squeegees. In these categories, there are many types and sizes of each available, and it is not possible to be too specific. However the following will provide some guidelines to use in selecting such tools.

When buying brushes, make sure the handles are BARE UNPAINTED WOOD. If the handles are painted, chances are the resin will eat off the paint and it will be tracked along in the resin causing a mess. With plastic handles, the resin may attack the plastic and soften it or even dissolve it. Don't use old paint brushes either as the resin may attack the old paint within the brush and mess up the resin. Use new brushes or well-cleaned brushes previously used with the same type of resin that you'll be using.

All brushes should have NATURAL bristles which are fairly stiff. You can often cut the bristles of a brush short to make it stiffer. Here again, natural bristles are specified because the resin may attack and soften many synthetic bristle types. Don't worry about getting fine quality bristles as they are usually too flexible anyhow, and

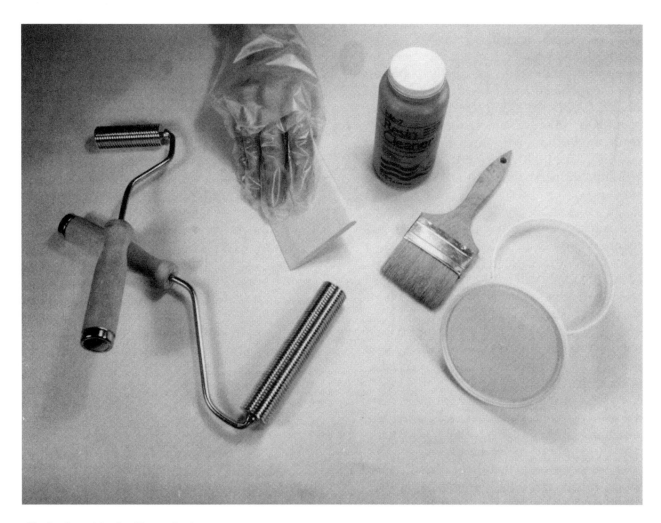

Hand tools used for sheathing applications are simple and inexpensive. The photo shows some of these including protective gloves, squeegee, natural bristle brush with unpainted wood handle, bar-rier cream for skin protection, and mat rollers (only required if working with mat). Not shown (but required) would be a typical paint roller handle with thin foam roller elements.

you'll probably wind up throwing the brush away when you're done. In short, get the cheapest, fairly stiff, short, natural bristle brush available with a plain unpainted wood handle. A brush width from 3″ to 4″ is usually most versatile.

Many types of roller elements can be used in applying resin similar to those used to apply paint. Probably the most common type is the ordinary mohair paint roller, which is not desirable, especially those with thicker naps. Other types are the foam roller elements which are preferable, but the conditions for selecting the best ones require some elaboration.

First, use foam rollers with cardboard cores unless you are sure that the core material (often plastic) will not be attacked by the resin. Second, not all foam rollers are compatible with resin, especially polyester resin, which can attack certain foams. If in doubt, check out a sample. Third, the special foam rollers often recommended for resin application with the thinnest foam coverings are highly desirable, especially if working with epoxy resins. The reasons are several.

Thin foam rollers entrap less air, which can cause undue stipling and air entrapment in the coating. Thin rollers allow a smoother surface than thicker covers. Finally, the foam will tend to hold resin, and the thicker the foam on the roller element, the more resin it will hold. While this may seem desirable at first, the problem is that once the resin sets up in the roller, it is wasted. At the price of resins, this can add up to a considerable expense if the roller traps a lot of resin that sets up and does not get used. Besides, the thicker rollers usually cost more in themselves. In any case, keep a good supply of rollers handy.

In selecting roller handles, consider one which can be fitted with an extension handle if you are involved in a project having expansive surface areas that may be hard to reach. Again, roller handles of wood are recommended, and keep in mind that the

resin can attack certain plastic parts of roller handles. If in doubt, make a test, but keep in mind for all of the preceding that with regard to resin attacking plastic, polyester is usually more of a culprit in this regard than epoxies, which usually do not have the solvents that cause these problems.

For applying fiberglass mat, a metal serrated disc roller, or "mat roller" as it is called, is ideal. They are not cheap, but are worth the money if your work with mat is extensive. They come in many sizes and shapes for use on flat surfaces, and outside and inside corners. Most come with unpainted wood handles suitable for fitting extensions. The reason these are used is that mat will tear and shred to pieces using tools ordinarily used for applying fiberglass cloth.

Squeegees come in many sizes and materials also. The type for cleaning windows is often used as long as the rubber part will not be attacked by the resin. Some of these can be fitted with extensions, but the hand-held type are usually preferable since they allow a better "feel" to the work. Other handheld squeegees are often simply pieces of plastic or rubber-like materials that can be immersed in solvent with no detriment. A size about 3″ × 6″ wide is good for most boat work, although a wider one may be more suitable for large areas. Some are available with tapered edges, radiused corners, or other specialized shapes for difficult-to-squeegee areas. They're all usually inexpensive and a couple of standard types per person doing the work will usually suffice (one can be kept in solvent ready for a fresh batch of resin while the other is in use).

PROTECTIVE CLOTHING & GEAR

The hazards and recommendations in regard to personnel protection when working with resins have been covered in Chapter

5, with emphasis in other portions of the text where applicable. Keep in mind also that some consideration should be given to handling the fiberglass materials themselves. Some people are not affected by handling fiberglass, while others just can't stand to be around the stuff in any form. Some people break out in rashes and scratch and itch for a week or more afterward. Most people have a reaction somewhere between these two extremes. Thus skin exposure should be kept to a minimum, especially around fiberglass mat where the fibers come loose easily.

In all cases, provide protective clothing and gear for safety and comfort. These items include protective gloves of the proper type to suit the resin being used, barrier cream and skin cleaners, face masks or goggles, and clothing that will keep resin from contacting the skin directly in the event of spills. Some of the inexpensive paper disposable protective clothing items now available (such as aprons, smocks, etc.) are ideal in this regard.

When working with resin, use the oldest and sloppiest junk clothing available because you will probably end up throwing it all away when the job is done. Cured resin cannot be removed from clothing, and liquid resin is also difficult to remove. Also wear shoes that offer good protection; certain fabric or canvas shoes can allow resin to soak through, which is not good protection. However, keep in mind that the shoes worn when working with resin will probably be ruined in the process.

MIXING CONTAINERS & EQUIPMENT

The type and sophistication of your mixing containers and equipment will vary with the type of resin being used, the extent of your project, and perhaps your budget.

For mixing polyester resin, things are pretty simple. While you can buy special mixing containers, probably one of the best and cheapest containers is a plastic bleach or ammonia bottle with the top portion cut off. Most of these are not affected by resin or solvents. These are nice since once the resin cures, it will break free from the container so it can be used again and again. However, don't leave too much unused resin in them since the heat from exotherm can melt them.

Plain paper mixing containers as well as wax paper cups and old CLEAN coffee cans are also suitable. Don't try to use Styrofoam containers or other plastic drinking cups for mixing polyester resin as the resin will fall right through the bottom. These plastics are dissolved by styrene as well as acetone and other solvents.

With epoxy resins, similar containers can be used, but from a safety standpoint (to avoid spills), they should be somewhat more substantial. Heavy-walled plastic containers with smooth surfaces are preferable (e.g. paint buckets). For epoxy, better plastic containers are sometimes available that are metered so that mixing the resin and hardener in the proper ratios is easy and foolproof. For large projects, resin metering pumps are available, but the added expense is seldom worth it.

With epoxy resins, similar containers can be used, but from a safety standpoint (to avoid spills), they should be somewhat more substantial. Heavy-walled plastic containers with smooth surfaces are preferable (e.g. paint buckets). For epoxy, better plastic containers are sometimes available that are metered so that mixing the resin and hardener in the proper ratios is easy and foolproof. For large projects, resin metering pumps are available, but the added expense is seldom worth it.

A problem with cut-off plastic bottles is that the insides are not always smooth, and this makes proper mixing (critical with epoxy) difficult. Similarly, ALL containers for either epoxy or polyester should be round for easier stirring. While plastic coated milk cartons may hold resin, the hard, square corners make thorough mixing (especially with epoxies) difficult; don't use these. Do NOT use glass or any type of breakable containers; these are too dangerous for practical use.

In any case, have enough containers to do the job. For example, with polyester resin, figure on at least four one-gallon cut-off bleach bottles (or comparable) per each gallon of resin, since a quart of resin at a time is all that most inexperienced workers will be able to work once the resin has been catalyzed. With epoxy resin, quantities are usually less, with a quart being about the maximum to ever mix up at a time. In either case, have a plentiful supply of stirring sticks from clean, plain wood that you can make up yourself. USE A FRESH NEW STIRRING STICK FOR EACH RESIN BATCH.

Once resin has been mixed with catalyst or hardener, it's often dispensed into paint trays. These should be lined with heavy plastic wrap or aluminum foil. Also, most paint stores have pre-formed disposable plastic liners which are ideal. These make roller application easy and disperse the resin to prevent heat build-up for a prolonged pot life.

CLEAN-UP

First and foremost, clean up efforts will be easiest and safest if measures are taken in advance to allow for the inevitable spills. Plan ahead! Cured resin spilled onto concrete is almost impossible to remove short of burning or melting it off, which can be hazardous. If you want to protect the floor or ground, old newspapers or rolls of kraft paper will often suffice. Plastic tarps can be slippery and dangerous; don't use these. Scrap pieces of plywood or hardboard are good, and swatches of fiberglass wetted out with resin can be used to anchor these together to prevent movement. This method

also protects dropped tools from damage.

Acetone is probably the most common cleaning solvent used for fiberglass work, but it's so volatile and evaporates so fast, large quantities can disappear quickly, and it's expensive. Although old fiberglass workers have used the stuff for skin cleaning purposes for years, DON'T!

A less volatile cleaning solvent is lacquer thinner, and many think it works better than acetone. But it's not cheap either, and skin contact should also be avoided. As with all solvents, read and take heed of all the precautionary information on the labels, particularly with regard to fire hazards. NEVER expose any solvents to bare skin, especially if they are contaminated with resin. They will tend to dry the protective oils from the skin, thereby opening the pores and allowing even easier passage of the solvents and the resin into the body's system.

Remember that if you are using cheap brushes and rollers, it will probably be cheaper to throw these away after use and use new ones, rather than attempt to clean them for reuse; the solvent used to clean an old tool could be more costly than the new one.

Better and safer cleaning agents are available under various trade names, with some commonly referred to as "resin cleaners" or "resin emulsifiers". While fairly expensive, these usually require little to do the job, and they save on the amount of solvents used. Otherwise, keep a pail of water around with ordinary detergent and/or household ammonia to wash up hands and tools after cleaning in solvents or resin cleaners.

MISCELLANEOUS EQUIPMENT

Use an old pair of scissors to cut fiberglass materials. Don't use a good pair since cutting fiberglass will dull the edges rapidly. Besides that, it is easy to get resin into the blades and jam them if you're not careful, especially when working with epoxies. Also get a good utility knife for trimming overhanging edges of fiberglass before the resin sets up.

A staple gun and/or tacks will come in handy for tacking fiberglass materials in position. Masking tape and old newspapers can be used to mask off an area so resin won't run onto surfaces where it is not intended. If a high gloss surface will be desired, such as for a clear natural wood finish, a buffer and accessories may be desired.

If the job must be done in cold temperatures (say anywhere less than 60°), try to heat the area. You can use portable heaters, heat lamps, or even bare bulbs will help a tremendous amount, especially when focused onto the surfaces to be sheathed. Beware of the hazards of fire, however, in these situations. Finally, don't forget the fire extinguisher.

TOOL & EQUIPMENT LIST

The following tools and equipment are used for various sheathing applications using fiberglass materials and resins. While the list is fairly comprehensive, not all the items will be required for each and every job. For example, if sheathing is being done over a new hull, there will be no need for paint remover. Similarly, if mat will not be used, there will be no need for a mat roller. Also, many will have a definite preference as to the type of sander they want to work with; thus it may not be necessary to have one of each type. The list may also vary depending on the size of the job, the types of materials being used, the type of surface being worked on, and to suit the desires of the worker. Consult the text for more details on options and alternatives best suited to the particular job at hand.

TOOL AND EQUIPMENT LIST

Paint remover, water base
Belt sander with several sanding belts
Disc sander with assorted sanding discs and foam disc pad
Finish sander, reciprocating or orbital
Sandpaper, assortment of grits
Sanding block
Sanding mask
Wood rasps, files, plane, or other surface-forming tools
Putty knife
Non-oil base filler or putty, or supplies to make your own
Brushes, natural bristle, bare wood handles, 3" to 4" wide
Rollers, foam paint type with matching roller handle frame
Mat roller, metal serrated type
Squeegees
Gloves, protective and/or disposable type
Barrier cream
Protective clothing, disposable or discardable type
Eye protection glasses, goggles, or face mask
Paint trays with liners
Mixing containers
Cleaning solvent (see text)
Resin cleaner solution
Detergent and/or household ammonia and water with bucket
Scissors
Utility knife or razor blade knife with spare blades
Staple gun, tacks, or masking tape
Newspaper or kraft paper
Stirring sticks, plain wood
Fire extinguisher, CLASS "B"
Portable heaters or heat lamps
Buffing equipment
Floor protection tarps or paper.

Before starting the actual process of fiber-glassing, it is necessary to have a properly prepared surface in order to assure sound results. Surface preparation is critical whether the sheathing will be done over a new or old boat regardless of the material the hull is built from or its method of planking. Because of the many variables in proper surface preparation, this chapter is broken down in sub-sections covering hull preparation principles for both new and old boats, suitability of wood planking systems for fiberglass sheathing application, types and uses of fillers used, and surface preparation of materials other than wood.

HULL PREPARATION – BASIC PRINCIPLES

The most critical step in the fiberglass sheathing process, whether the boat is new or old, is surface preparation. Take any shortcuts in this regard and the job can turn out a failure, not to mention a waste of time, money, and effort. The most basic principle, and one easy to overlook even on a new boat, is that fiberglass and resin MUST be applied ONLY to a surface that is clean, dry, and free of any dust contamination, old paint, varnish, oil, grease, paint or chemical spray residue, or dirt. Whether the substrate is wood, metal, or whatever, it should be BARE, CLEAN, AND DRY!

It is not necessary that the surface be perfectly smooth. In fact, a somewhat roughened or "scuffed" surface can increase mechanical "keying" of the resin to provide a better bond, and is thus recom-

mended. This is not to say that the surface can be unfair, however. Remember that any unfair surfaces will just be made worse in appearance with any laminate buildup. In other words, any lumps, bumps, or dips will be "telegraphed" to the surface and show up even worse once the hull is painted. Thus make sure that any surface to be sheathed is as fair to the touch and eye as is possible. Time spent in this process will be greatly rewarded in a "yacht-like" finish.

Finally, pick the sheathing materials that are BEST suited to your application, using the information presented. Follow instructions in this book, and as provided with the products used, to the letter. Do NOT make any deviations except on the advice of experts.

SUITABILITY OF WOOD PLANKING SYSTEMS

Whether or not a wood boat is a candidate for a fiberglass sheathing application depends somewhat on whether the boat is new or old, but mainly on the type and soundness of its planking method and underlying structure.

Sheathing of wood boats with fiberglass is most satisfactorily done on stable hull types; that is, planking methods which are in a sense rigid and don't move at the seams. Ordinarily, such boats are those glued with hard-setting glues. These planking methods include sheet plywood planking, strip planking, multi-layered veneer or "cold molded" hulls, and combination strip planked/veneer hulls.

Boats planked in the conventional "plank-on-frame" methods, such as carvel, batten seam, or lapstrake, can be attempted with varying degrees of success depending on the resins used and other options, in particular consideration of sheathing materials other than fiberglass as discussed in PART 2 of this book.

The latter planking methods are sensitive to moisture changes; the planks tend to shrink when the boat is removed from the water, and to expand when the boat is returned to the water. Consequently there is the tendency for any sheathing material to split and crack at the seams and possibly delaminate. Also, some woods contain acids or oils which make resin bonding difficult or questionable.

However, judging the stability of a particular planking method's suitability for a sheathing application, particularly on old boats, is subjective and perhaps difficult. If in doubt, you may want to consult a marine surveyor or naval architect for a recommendation. The type of wood used for the planking (some expand and contract more than others), severity of service, and other factors already discussed must all be considered to make sure the sheathing application is worth the time, work, and expense when older boats are being considered.

In all wood planking systems based on "plank-on-frame" techniques, any sheathing materials applied should be done with an epoxy resin except in the case of the C-FLEX Sheathing System described in Chapter 14. This will assure the most positive bond and prevent the tendency for delamination even if the sheathing material does crack at a seam. Furthermore, if in doubt about the movement of such a hull, one of the other sheathing materials, such as polypropylene or modacrylic fabrics, should be considered in lieu of fiberglass (see Chapters 10 and 11).

HULL PREPARATION – OLD WOOD BOATS

To make the fiberglass and resin application easier, and to assure proper results, remove ALL appendages such as skegs, external keels, rubbing strakes, and rails, if possible. Also remove all hardware such as mooring cleats, metal rub rails, underwater hardware and fittings, etc. Remember that resin will only adhere over a clean, dry, bare wood surface. This means that ALL existing paint, varnish, marine growth, oil, grease, and dirt must be removed.

The BEST method (but NOT the easiest!) is to sand with coarse sandpaper, using portable power sanders. The fastest sanders are disc and belt sanders, but they require careful handling; finish sanders are usually impractical for this use. While sandblasting can be attempted, many operators frown on this since it's easy to remove a considerable amount of wood in short order, especially with softwoods. If any sandblasting is done, make sure all the dust and sand are removed, wash down the surfaces, and allow them to dry thoroughly prior to doing the sheathing work.

On old boats planked with Douglas fir and other rotary-cut plywoods, there is a tendency to over-sand the surface, causing it to develop "hills" and "valleys" due to the grain pattern of the outer lamination. For a smooth, flat, level surface, such over-sanding must be avoided. Also, the outer veneers of some plywoods, particularly those with hardwood veneers, can be quite thin. Care should be taken not to sand through these.

A "water rinse" paint remover can be used to remove paint in conjunction with sanding, especially where the paint has a tenacious grip or many coats have been built up. However, do NOT use ordinary paint removers which contain waxes, oils, or other petroleum products as these can be absorbed into the wood and prevent proper bonding of the resin.

When using "water rinse" paint removers, be SURE that all traces of the remover are washed away as any residue can cause bonding problems. Surfaces can be washed with detergent and water, lye solution, acetone, or similar solvent. But be SURE the surface is ABSOLUTELY dry BEFORE applying resin and sheathing materials. Take particular care in using paint removal products since they are hazardous; follow label instructions and hazard warnings to the letter.

Do NOT attempt to use heat or flame (such as a blowtorch) to remove old paint. The heat will tend to drive any residual oils and solvents from the old paint and fuse them into the wood fibers, besides possibly charring the wood. Also, do NOT use oil- or petroleum-based solvents such as gasoline or paint thinners to remove oil or grease spots. Oil and grease should be removed with a mild solution of detergent and water or comparable cleaner that will not drive the contamination into the wood cells.

Remove all LOOSE putty and caulking

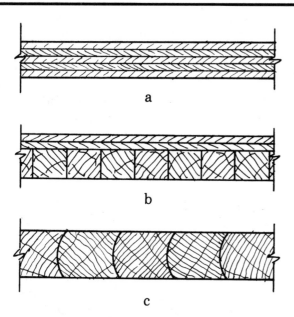

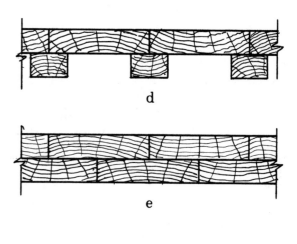

WOOD PLANKING TYPES & THEIR SUITABILITY FOR SHEATHING

The stability of the planking type has a large bearing on the successful outcome of the fiberglass sheathing. Wood planking methods which expand and contract with variations in moisture content are more prone to cracking and delamination than stable planking types.

The illustrations show common wood planking methods, with the most stable types at the top of the list. The order that the different planking methods are given is roughly the order of the degree of success that can be expected from a particular application. The judgement of the stability of a particular planking method is subjective and can vary considerably between actual boats depending on the type and quality of wood used, the boat's structural integrity, and service to which it is put.

(a) STABLE—Sheet plywood, double or multi-diagonal plywood strips or solid wood veneers, or so-called "cold molded", and "Ashcroft" planking methods present few problems. Two layers of cloth or a layer each of mat and cloth may be desirable where service is severe or on larger boats. Otherwise, a single layer of cloth usually suffices using either polyester or epoxy resin.

(b) STABLE—Strip planked/wood veneer using thin solid wood veneers in a double diagonal format on the outside over a strip planked base that has been edge-glued. Can be considered similar to (a).

(c) STABLE—Strip planking, usually glued and edge fastened. The faying surface (joint between planks) may vary from that shown. Presents few problems and can be considered similar to (a).

(d) VARIABLE—Batten seam planking. Best results occur where planks are narrow, firmly backed up, and fastened, using good quality wood. Epoxy resin is advised. Two layers of cloth may yield better results.

materials, and tighten all loose planks and boards, replacing fastenings as necessary. All fastening holes and other minor imperfections should be filled with an oil-free hard-setting wood putty, or you can make your own, as will be described shortly, and this can be used for major filling and fairing operations also. All seams between planks on "plank-on-frame" hulls should be recaulked if old caulking is loose, followed by a non-oil seam compound after. Inspect for areas of rot, and if detected, the rotted area should be removed and replaced or otherwise repaired. So-called "rot repair" kits or

products are available for this purpose, but often using epoxy products on your own will suffice.

All crisp outside corners should be radiused as much as possible. With some boat styles this can be a problem and even a detriment to performance, however. For example, planked boats using the lapstrake or "clinker" method which present alternating inside and outside edges at each successive plank are extremely difficult if not impractical to cover with fiberglass cloth and resin unless each strake corner is gently radiused and each inside corner built up

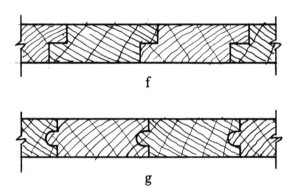

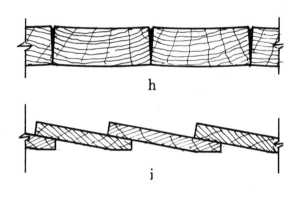

(e) VARIABLE—Double planked hulls. Best results occur where planks are narrow, of good quality wood, with both layers well bonded together and fastened to a sound structure. Epoxy resin is advised. Two layers of cloth may yield better results.

(f) VARIABLE—Shiplap planking. Not common for hulls but may be used on decks. Best results occur with narrow planks of good quality wood over a sound structure. Epoxy resin is advised along with two layers of cloth for best results.

(g) VARIABLE—Tongue-in-groove. Not commonly used for hull planking but may be used on decks. Same considerations as (f).

(h) UNSTABLE—Carvel planking. Wide planks, poor wood, cupping, severe contraction and expansion, and unsound structures which move and work are common problems which prevent a successful application using lighter weight materials. The method presented in Chapter 14 is one solution. Otherwise, epoxy resin should be used in conjunction with materials presented in Part 2.

(i) UNSTABLE—Lapstrake or "clinker" planking. Not recommended for use with fiberglass as hulls of this type tend to work

and flex too much. Wide planks, poor wood, cupping, severe expansion and contraction, and unsound structures are common problems. Covering alternating inside and outside corners of planks is virtually impractical unless fitted with generous radius and/or cant strips. Use epoxy resin and Dynel if done at all (see Chapter 11).

In any of the above wood planking methods, if there is any question regarding the stability of the wood planking method, it may be best to select a sheathing material such as "Vectra" or "Dynel" in conjunction with epoxy resin; these combinations will "stretch" more with the wood than fiberglass used with either polyester or epoxy resin. Or one may want to consider the sheathing system discussed in Chapter 14. If adhesion will be a potential problem, regardless of the planking method, epoxy resin is recommended regardless of the sheathing material (except if using the method described in Chapter 14 which is based on polyester resins).

with a small cant strip or fillet of resin putty filler material. On boats of this type, a lighter weight fiberglass cloth (say no more than 7½-ounce) might make the work easier, or use a more suitable material such as modacrylic fabric as described in Chapter 11. In any case, this application can be tedious.

On planked cabin tops and decks of old boats, such as those few still around which might be covered with canvas, attempting to remove the canvas adhesive may be futile; sanding may just gum up the paper. Furthermore, such planking may be cupped and warped, making sanding to a level surface even more difficult. A better solution may be to glue and fasten down a thin layer of plywood over the planked area. This eliminates these problems, saves time and work, and strengthens the deck or cabin top. A better, more positive, sheathing will also result.

At seams in the plywood, use a disc sander to create a shallow hollow at the butt joint about ¹⁄₁₆" deep and 6" wide. Fill this with fiberglass cloth strips, the first strip being 6" wide, and the second strip over this being 4" wide. Sand flush after

cure. For maximum strength, cut cloth strips on a 45° bias so strands cross the butt joint both ways. Although cloth may tend to unravel this way, there will be no parallel strands at the seam which result in no strength from the fibers that would be running in this direction.

On high-speed boats, such as hydroplanes, tunnel hulls, and other planing hulls, edges along the bottom, especially at the stern or along sponsons, should be kept as crisp as possible, although a method for making a crisp edge AFTER radiusing the corner and covering with fiberglass is described in Chapter 9. Inside corners, such as along the tunnels of multihulls, hydroplane sponsons, etc., should be fitted with wood cant strips, or a generously rounded fillet can be made using resin-putty filler.

In all cases where inside or outside corners occur, radiusing is necessary so the sheathing material will adhere to the surface and not lift, thereby forming air bubbles and avenues for water to penetrate under the sheathing. This statement applies to BOTH old and new boats.

One note of caution on plywood planked boats with relatively thin (say ¼" or less)

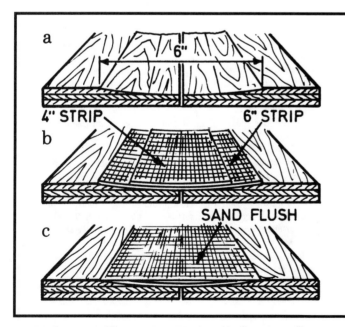

If thin plywood has been laid over a planked deck or cabin top, for example, to act as a substrate for a sheathing application, butt joints in the plywood should be made as shown. A disc sander can be used to create a slight concave depression about ¹⁄₁₆" deep along the joint about 6" wide. A couple of strips of cloth or tape (approximately 4" and 6" wide respectively) can then be applied to be level to the surface.

For even more strength, the cloth can be cut on the bias (at 45°) so the strands cross the junction in two directions. A bead of resin can be used to keep the cut material from unravelling at the cut edges (see text on how to make your own cloth tape). Sand the area level after curing and then apply the sheathing material; junctions in the sheathing should be located beyond the plywood butt joint.

planking; it is sometimes difficult to radius an outside corner enough as the fastenings may be in the way. It is also easy to take away too much of the plywood laminations, so be careful when radiusing outside corners on this type of planking.

TYPES AND USES OF FILLERS

In preparing the surface for a sheathing application, any indentations, fastening holes, imperfections, and unfair or sub-level areas must be filled and faired so a smooth, even surface develops. Also, certain areas of a hull may need to be built up with filler materials where it is expedient or impractical to fit in a wood member. A common situation where this occurs is at inside corners where the fiberglass would not otherwise adhere to the surface, but would lift and form air bubbles.

In using any filler material for these purposes, it MUST be an oil-free product that will dry hard, yet allow sanding and fairing to be performed with relative ease. Preferably such fillers will not tend to shrink or crack, and will stay bonded to the substrate surface as well as to the sheathing resin.

Many non-oil-based putties are available and suitable. There are those wood filler or wood putty products which are ready-to-use from the container and apply with a regular putty knife. Most can be thinned with acetone or lacquer thinner, or have their own recommended solvents. These are handy for filling screw holes and minor imperfections since they dry quickly, sand easily, and bond well. Some products of this type come in various wood color tints so they can be used for natural finish work. However, they don't work as well for larger blemishes that may be deep or extend over a broad area.

Other fillers are available as two-part mixes based on polyester or epoxy formulations that can be mixed together for immediate use. Some of these consist of resin

thickened with silica and/or talc additives. Others include an addition of chopped or milled strands of fiberglass for reinforcing purposes. Many of these products are used in auto bodywork and have their place in marine use as well. While they are convenient, these ready-made products are not always inexpensive nor as workable as they could be in various situations encountered in sheathing preparation work.

MAKING YOUR OWN FILLERS

Although ready-made products may be convenient and suitable, there is no reason why you cannot make your own fillers, and there are plenty of reasons why you should. The main reason to make your own filler is that you can make up any amount desired at any time needed in any consistency you deem suitable.

You can nearly duplicate many of the ready-made filler products described above just by adding some silica filler and perhaps some chopped up strands of fiberglass to some resin. Some people even use resin or glue mixtures with sawdust or talc. A problem with these and many ready-made products is that they are not always easy to sand nor light in weight. However, making your own more suitable filler is fast and easy once you get a "feel" for the suitable consistency you need.

Either polyester or epoxy resin can be used; the same one you'll be using for the sheathing application will usually suffice. While you can make your filler with either polyester or epoxy resin, if your sheathing application will be with epoxy resin, use ONLY epoxy resin for your filler in this instance.

In addition to the resin, you'll need a filler material, many types of which are available, but most are similar. These products are commonly known as "microspheres", a generic name for microscopically thin, hollow, gas-filled balls or bal-

47

loons often available under trade names such as "Microballoons", "Glass Beads", "Q-Cell", "Gericell", etc., depending on the manufacturer. Most are made from silica (glass), phenolic, or other forms of plastic.

Microspheres come in a fine powder form of very low density and very light weight. When mixed with the resin, they extend the resin and increase the viscosity. When

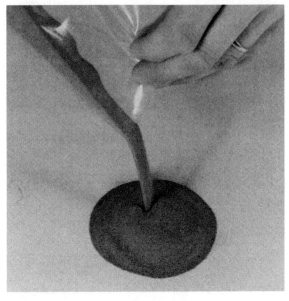

Microsphere products come in several varieties. The tiny gas-filled bubbles have the consistency of fine-grained sand, flour, or dust, and are very light in weight. Always wear a dust mask when working with these.

added in high volumes, a "syntactic foam" (another term for a resin which has been "stretched out") forms that is ideal for fairing and filling operations. Because the filler materials are mostly air, they sand easily and are lightweight once the resin cures.

Mixing up a batch of filler is pretty much guesswork and will vary somewhat with the type of filler material, resin viscosity, ambient temperatures, etc. It is difficult at first to estimate how much will be needed to do an area also, so some experimentation is always called for at first. Just remember that a little filler goes a long way and the tendency is to begin with too much resin initially; start off with a minimal amount of resin.

Some manufacturers of microspheres give recommendations regarding mixes. For example, one company says that a 5% concentration BY WEIGHT is trowelable, and that a 10% concentration is "very viscous". However, when working in small amounts, figuring out 5% or 10% of the filler material by weight would require a very accurate scale capable of measuring in small quantities; this is impractical.

Easier mixing can be done BY VOLUME, and experience with some of the products does provide some guidelines, at least to start with. For a trowelable mix, such as would be used for making a fillet, try a ratio of 2½ TO 3 PARTS FILLER TO 1 PART RESIN BY VOLUME. These proportions can be varied plus or minus to suit without adverse affects, yielding what is called a "low-density" filleting material.

Some microspheres are a little rough to apply; that is, they may tend to drag and leave a surface that should be smoother and fairer. One way to make a mixture that is smoother, easier to apply, and permits easier feathering or smoothing at edges, is to add some silica, the same type used to make a polyester resin thixotropic.

However, depending on the amount of silica added, the tendency is to increase the density and weight, and make the surface somewhat harder to sand. Amounts of as small as one part silica to nine parts microspheres show noticeable improvement. For a mix that works well for improved filleting, first BLEND DRY 1 PART FILLER + 1 PART SILICA FILLER, then add this at 2½ TO 3 PARTS FILLER BLEND TO 1 PART RESIN BY VOLUME. Minor variations are acceptable as required. For fillet work, a peanut butter consistency works well.

As noted, ambient temperatures can also affect the ratios somewhat; warmer temperatures may cause the mix to thin out or "sag" somewhat from exotherm also as the mixture sets up. One way to minimize this is to work the mix as long as practical. In the case of polyester resin, a bit more catalyst can be added to speed the reaction. However, keep in mind that filler mixes tend to capture more heat than resin alone, and this can speed curing. Therefore, start out with small batches and experiment.

It is important to note that filler mixing procedures vary from polyester to epoxy resins. With polyester resins, the filler can be added to the resin first and the catalyst added after. This gives plenty of time to blend the resin and filler material, but make sure the catalyst is mixed THOROUGHLY! Of course, if you can work fast enough, you could add the catalyst first, but working time would be decreased to perhaps an impractical limit. In either case, add catalyst only to suit the amount of resin used initially. Because sanding will be done over just about any cured filler mix, the polyester resin should be a finishing type or one with surfacing agent added; using laminating resin will make sanding difficult.

With epoxy resins, because the hardener portion is usually a substantial percentage of the resin/hardener mix, and because thorough mixing of the two components is more critical than with polyesters, the filler should be added AFTER the resin and hardener have been mixed. To allow as much mixing time as possible, an epoxy formulation with a "slow" hardener should be

used if available to allow a longer pot life.

Regardless of the resin used, mechanical mixing is generally not advised. This can damage the individual microspheres or cause them to "collapse", lessening their value and qualities. Mixing small batches by hand is preferable. Add a little filler material at a time rather than attempt to stir it all in at once. Also, ALWAYS WEAR A PROTECTIVE DUST MASK when pouring and mixing these products.

For clear natural finished sheathed surfaces, most microsphere materials used underneath are opaque and have a color. Some are white and are therefore noticeable. Others are a brown tint that come close to matching some types of wood, and are therefore less obvious. Sawdust has also been used by some for this affect.

FILLER APPLICATION & MAKING FILLETS

A fillet is a radiused bead at the inside of two joining panels. In some types of wood boat construction, these fillets are structural in nature (as in so-called "stitch-and-glue" boats), or may be used to bond adjoining members (such as bulkhead junctions) in place. Epoxy resin is recommended in these cases because of superior bonding strength and other physical qualities derived from the resin. In other cases, the fillet merely keeps the fiberglass sheathing from lifting from the surface as it would if the fillet were absent; either type of resin is suitable in this case, although polyester resin also adds considerable strength.

Fillets can be made in various sizes depending on their function. However, when they become large, two or more progressive applications are more successful than trying to build up a large fillet at one time. If using polyester resin in this instance, make the first application with laminating resin, allowing the first to set up somewhat, and the second application with finishing resin

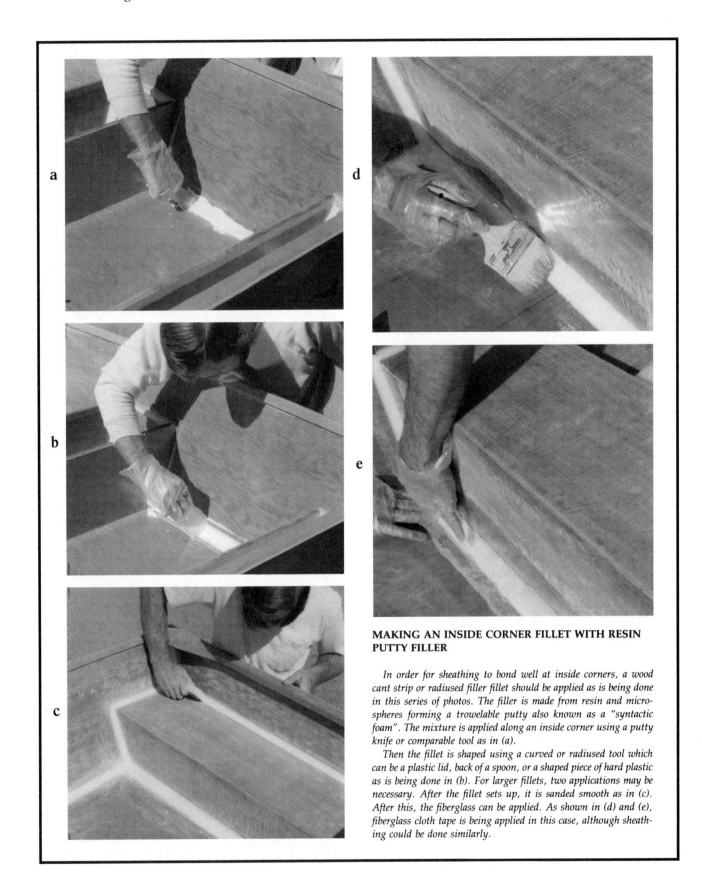

MAKING AN INSIDE CORNER FILLET WITH RESIN PUTTY FILLER

In order for sheathing to bond well at inside corners, a wood cant strip or radiused filler fillet should be applied as is being done in this series of photos. The filler is made from resin and microspheres forming a trowelable putty also known as a "syntactic foam". The mixture is applied along an inside corner using a putty knife or comparable tool as in (a).

Then the fillet is shaped using a curved or radiused tool which can be a plastic lid, back of a spoon, or a shaped piece of hard plastic as is being done in (b). For larger fillets, two applications may be necessary. After the fillet sets up, it is sanded smooth as in (c). After this, the fiberglass can be applied. As shown in (d) and (e), fiberglass cloth tape is being applied in this case, although sheathing could be done similarly.

for easier sanding after cure.

A small fillet is easier to form if it contains a good percentage of silica, and it will be stronger than using microspheres alone. It is possible for a fillet to be too big. Basically this point is reached when it would be easier to fit a wood cant strip rather than attempt to make the successive fillet applications necessary using a resin putty. Also, big fillets become increasingly labor intensive and expensive, and may add more weight than a wood cant strip.

Some practice is necessary before nice, smooth fillets can be made quickly. On wood surfaces, precoat the area with resin (laminating resin in the case of polyesters) and let them set up a bit before applying the fillet. If the surface cures, sand lightly first. Several tools can be used to position the fillet mixture including cake decorating tools, syringes, squeeze bottles, cartridge gun blanks, or just scoop in place. Any round object can do the shaping such as tongue depressors or plastic lids of suitable radius (these can be used over and over since the resin does not stick to them). Try to make your fillets as smooth as possible initially; this will save considerable sanding work later. Once the fillet has cured, it can be sanded smooth.

For other uses, filler materials can be used to build up unfair areas, especially low spots. In these cases, the filler mixture can be thinner (except on vertical surfaces), perhaps the consistency of a thick pancake batter. The mix can be spread with many tools such as a drywall knife, firm squeegee, notched trowel, etc. After curing, sanding can take place to fair the area and then sheathing can be applied.

SURFACE PREPARATION OVER MATERIALS OTHER THAN WOOD

In boat work, other materials over which fiberglass may be applied include aluminum, steel, ferro-cement (concrete), and even fiberglass. However, modern technology has advanced the quality and durability of coating systems and construction methods used in building boats from these materials to the point where covering such surfaces entirely with fiberglass would largely be a waste of time, work, and money.

However, there may be some occasion or need where a covering of limited area, or the use of a related product (such as a filler), might be considered, as is repair purposes. For example, metal hulls which have become dented or otherwise deformed in localized areas can often be brought back to shape with a combination of ordinary auto body repair techniques to reshape the area, and a surface filling of an epoxy filler used to smooth out the area. In other cases, a person may want to encapsulate a steel centerboard in fiberglass to protect it from rust and corrosion, or fiberglass may be used to make a repair on an existing fiberglass hull or deck.

Except in the case of fiberglass repairs over fiberglass boats, epoxy resins should be used in all cases rather than polyester resin on surfaces other than wood. Even then, epoxies are optional in lieu of polyester resin on existing fiberglass boats if fiberglass cloth is being used for the work, as it will bond tenaciously to the existing polyester laminate.

Although boat repair as such is not the subject of this text, the most important step in the application of fiberglass to surfaces other than wood is again surface preparation. In the case of fiberglass boats, surfaces should be taken down below any gel coats but short of cutting into the laminate as such. As with wood, surfaces must be clean and dry.

In the case of metal hulls and parts where epoxy resin is required, surface preparation can become complicated and complex. Most metals oxidize rapidly when exposed to air. With aluminum, an oxide layer develops which adheres tightly to the metal. With steel, oxidation results in a loose oxide layer (rust) which makes a poor bonding base. If possible, contact the resin supplier for any special recommendation for bonding to metals.

In either case, several methods can be used and new processes may be in development. Those described in the following may not be the only suitable methods, and not all methods may be suitable to all users, especially the novice amateur. In all cases, proper safety precautions should be taken, especially when handling acids or solvents of any kind. Because of the specialized nature of some of these products, it may be best to turn such work over to a professional familiar with their safe and proper handling.

Solvent wipes or degreasing as noted in the following can be done with trichlorethylene, perchlorethylene, or lacquer thinner. However, keep in mind that these materials involve personal hazards which should be protected against. With solvent wipes, use a second clean cotton rag to pick up residues in all cases while the surface is still wet with solvent.

Aluminum can be prepared by several methods, some simple, others complex and perhaps beyond the beginner. While a bond will result with only a solvent wipe, bond strength will increase considerably with the addition of surface abrasion, such as sanding, sandblasting, grinding, or filing. More involved systems include an acid etch in a solution of concentrated sulfuric acid (10 parts by weight), distilled water (30 parts by weight), and sodium dichromate (1 part by weight) at 180°F for 10 minutes. Rinse thoroughly and dry. In either method, apply resin within three hours. Do NOT touch the surface with bare hands.

With steel, degrease and sandblast, grind, file, or sand the surface to bare metal and degrease again. Alternately, an acid etch in a solution of 25% sodium dichromate and 75% concentrated sulfuric acid can be done for 15 minutes at room temperature. In either case, apply resin within one hour.

CHAPTER 9

How To Do The Job

GETTING READY

The most important factor leading to a successful fiberglassing job is ORGANIZATION. It's surprising how many fiberglassing jobs have been botched up simply because a little forethought was not done before the job got underway. A little careful planning at this stage can help assure that everything will go smoothly once the work begins. Remember, once catalyst or hardener is mixed with the resin, it's on its way to cure and won't wait for you if it is necessary to run around looking for a brush or roller that has suddenly been misplaced. So plan ahead!

For such planning, a checklist of EVERYTHING that will be required is often desirable. Such a checklist can be tailored to suit your requirements or desires, using the information provided in earlier chapters. The points below can be used to help prepare for the job ahead. And to instill confidence to those who have never worked with fiberglass materials before, remember that if instructions are followed, it is almost impossible to make a mistake WHICH CANNOT BE CORRECTED. With proper planning, most errors can be prevented before they do occur.

1. Have all tools and supplies ready to go and handy. Try to have a proper place for everything, arranged so the fiberglass materials will remain clean and dry, and not become inadvertently soiled, wet, or spattered with resin. Have plenty of everything you'll need so it won't be necessary to stop and chase around for something when it might be needed the most.

2. Take time to PROPERLY prepare the surface as noted previously. Check the surface carefully so it won't be necessary to fill a screw hole or other imperfection that was somehow overlooked and now spotted AFTER the resin has been mixed. For ease of application, try to have the hull upsidedown if covering a hull. The more horizontal a surface is, the easier the application and the better the surface will come out with less work.

3. Pick a suitable area to do the job. Do NOT work in direct sunlight; the heat will speed the cure, perhaps cause undue shrinkage, possibly affect the sanding qualities, or lead to other defects. If possible, do the work under cover, or at least in a shaded area. In areas where moisture from fog, dew, or rain may settle on the surface overnight, work should be done indoors or at least be protected from this occurrence. Have plenty of ventilation and good light, but avoid extreme fan-forced air circulation devices or windy conditions which might dry solvents from the resin too rapidly. Also avoid working in areas where surface contamination from neighboring activities (such as paint overspray, oil mists, spray pesticides, etc.) might occur.

4. Pick the best weather conditions possible and allow enough time to do the

job. Start as early in the morning as possible, with temperatures ranging between 70°F and 85°F, and with as low humidity as possible (absolutely no rain if working outdoors). If the work must be done in colder temperatures, use a resin specially suited to such conditions. Colder temperatures can otherwise increase viscosity and difficulty of saturation, leading to numerous problems. If the temperature is OVER 85°F, take steps given in previous chapters to slow down pot life and cure times, and plan on working faster.

5. Cut and fit (or otherwise check) material BEFORE application to at least rough oversize in order to make sure there will be enough material to do the job just in case you estimated incorrectly. This will also verify that your supplier did not make a mistake. Also check your fiberglass for any defective areas or short lengths where joints or patches may thereby become necessary; this will prevent any unexpected "surprises" as material is rolled out or unfolded. The material, however, can be cut to exact size afterward as will be noted later.

6. With polyester resin, mark the catalyst container in increments in some manner if this has not been done by the manufacturer. One way to do this is to put a strip of masking tape on the container and mark off equal increments for the number of resin batches that will be used per container of resin.

7. Pour the container of resin into smaller mixing containers of equal increments. One quart of resin is about as much as can be used by ONE PERSON (less in the case of many epoxies) in a 20- to 30-minute period before the resin starts to gel. By having the resin divided before starting, a new batch can be cata-

lyzed or hardener added without delay so the application can be a continuous operation. For example, with each gallon of polyester resin, have no LESS than four mixing containers, each capable of holding a quart of resin each. If using epoxy resin, consider the mixing proportions and divide resin into containers that can also hold the proper amount of hardener. However, do NOT add catalyst or hardener at this time; just have the ingredients ready.

8. Have clean-up materials and equipment ready at all times. It is far easier to remove any resin before it begins to cure than after. If you feel that you'll need help, even if just for fitting and handling the cloth, have that person ready when needed, fully briefed and instructed on what will happen and what's expected.

ABOUT THIS CHAPTER

What follows in the balance of this chapter are the actual "how-to" methods of applying various fiberglass materials, using various combinations, alternatives, and options, with either polyester or epoxy resins AS THEY APPLY TO BOATS. For other applications, the procedures may be similar, and thus the material provided may give general guidance. However, if conditions of use are considerably different from those described, certain variations may be required.

Due to the many variables in methods, materials, and surface applications, it is not possible to provide so-called "step-by-step" procedures for every situation. What IS provided is the technical and practical information required to complete just about any project which entails the surface application or "sheathing" with fiberglass materials and resin. While most of the following information is basic to surface applications over wood or plywood, the principles are applicable to other materials properly prepared to which resin will bond.

In Chapter 4 the differences between polyester and epoxy resins were described, and these are the two basic types used for sheathing applications. Generally, each is applied and used in much the same way in sheathing applications. However, there are some difference in their selection and handling which will be noted in the following chapter. Therefore, BE SURE TO READ CAREFULLY WHICH RESIN IS BEING DISCUSSED AT ANY MOMENT WHERE A DISTINCTION IS MADE BETWEEN THE TWO TYPES. Otherwise, problems could occur.

POLYESTER RESIN SELECTION & HANDLING

In Chapter 4 describing polyester resins, it was emphasized that there are two types of polyester resins; those which contain wax (called "finishing" resin), and those which do NOT contain wax (called "laminating" resin). During a fiberglass sheathing application, several coats of resin will be applied to complete the job, and because of this, some polyester resin suppliers have developed so-called resin "systems" designed for the sequential application of the various coats of resin that will be required.

For example, one supplier may "formulate" three resins for his "system" (one for each coat) which he may label accordingly. The first resin he might call a "bonding" resin, which would be for the initial coat. The second resin may be called a "flow coat" resin which would be used to build up the resin thickness. These two resins would probably not contain wax since sanding would not ordinarily be done at these stages. The third resin may be called "sanding" resin for the final coat, and would therefore contain wax, plus perhaps some ingredient or filler supposedly to aid

sanding.

Another supplier may have a similar group of products, but call them by other names. In either instance, a purchase of several different resins would be suggested, which could lead to leftover material and a waste of money. But is this necessary? The whole point is that all this variety often tends to confuse and mystify the beginner and probably add to the cost. Regardless of what a supplier calls his polyester products, the resin will either contain wax or it will not.

Keep this point in mind: Any covering work can be done with EITHER laminating OR finishing resin as long as certain rules are followed. It IS, however, EASIER to use laminating resin than finishing resin for all but finish coats.

Remember that the wax in the finishing resin is used to "lock out" the air so the resin will set up hard. The wax rises to the surface due to the heat generated during the cure. This wax MUST be removed in order to obtain a good bond for additional coats of resin if required. The ONLY way to remove this wax practically is by sanding. Keep in mind that the wax is "greasy" and resin won't bond to grease as noted in previous chapters.

But is all the preceding TOTALLY correct? Not quite; there is a technical "contingency" based on the fact that WITHIN ABOUT A TWO HOUR PERIOD under normal application temperatures, the wax is still fluid or "soft" enough so that additional coats of resin containing wax can be applied directly to the initial coat without bonding problems AS LONG AS THE SURFACE IS LIBERALLY AND VIGOROUSLY WIPED DOWN WITH SOLVENT such as acetone or lacquer thinner.

By applying the second resin coat within this time period, the wax is still able to float through to the surface of the next coat. However, if a longer period transpires before applying the next coat (for example, within a day or two), not only should the surface be washed down with solvent, but it should be sanded as well to remove the wax, as it will be hard by this time. The reason for washing down the surface is that it makes sanding easier, keeps the paper from loading up so much, and prevents the heat generated during sanding from driving the wax back into the surface. After washing the surface with solvent, it will tend to be tacky, but this soon disappears, and the surface will seem hard again.

Since it is difficult on an object as large as some boats may be to keep applying resin within the two-hour limit, the preceding should not be considered "normal procedure". This method is primarily described as a "tip" for the person who may only have finishing resin to work with for one reason or another, and the project or area involved is not large. If finishing resin is improperly used, successive coats over it will not bond; after curing, it will be possible to scrape or chip these coats from the wax-coated surface. Such a practice will lead to failure in use.

It is still recommended that the surface coated with finishing resin be sanded, at least lightly, as it will assure a positive bond between the resin and fiberglass material when finishing resin may be used for all coats. The problem with this is that on initial coats used to first bond and wet out the fiberglass, the resin coat will probably not be thick enough to conceal the weave of the fiberglass cloth. If it is sanded, there will be a tendency to cut into the cloth, and this should not occur.

Therefore, a laminating resin is preferable for all but finish coats. Laminating resin contains no wax, and because of this, the surface will not cure COMPLETELY in the presence of air (at least the forseeable near-term), and will not require sanding. Especially on a warm day, or if over-catalyzed, surfaces coated with laminating resin may seem to have cured after many hours. But there will always be a certain degree of tackiness remaining which can be

checked by pushing hard with your thumb or thumbnail. This quality of laminating resin allows successive coats of resin to be applied with no surface preparation or sanding, provided the surface has not been contaminated by dirt, dust, grease, etc. If some time does transpire before applying the next coat, it is a good idea to wipe the surface with solvent just in case of any surface contamination which could interfere with the bond of the next coat.

POLYESTER RESIN FINISH COATS

In fiberglass covering work, the final resin coat (often called the "finish", "surface", or "sanding" coat) must be allowed to cure, and it is for this reason that finish resin containing wax is usually used for this coat. However, laminating resin can still be used for this coat also BY DOING ONE OF TWO THINGS.

Obviously, to have the resin surface cure, the air must be "locked out". One way to do this when the final coat of laminating resin has been applied is to spray or brush the partially cured surface with polyvinyl alcohol solution (or "PVA"). An even coating of PVA is not important, and once the resin cures completely (give it a day or two), the PVA, which is water soluble, is washed off.

PVA is a mold release agent commonly used in fiberglass female molding work in production situations. Thus it may be difficult to find at the retail level in nominal amounts. Furthermore, it is a "red label" product because of high flammability and cannot be shipped by mail or parcel service.

The second (and for most, the PREFERABLE) way to "lock out" the air using laminating resin for the final coat is to put the wax in the resin yourself! This way ONE resin (laminating resin) can be used THROUGHOUT the fiberglass sheathing application, making your own finish resin in just the quantity needed when it's

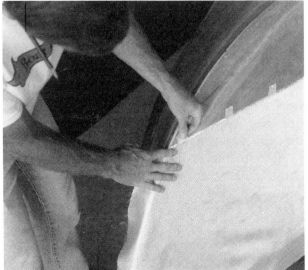
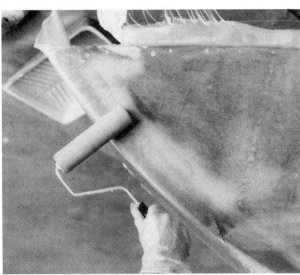
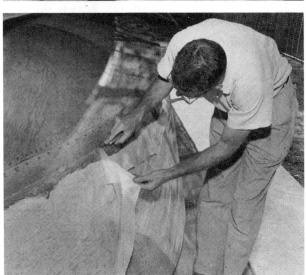

COVERING A BOAT HULL WITH FIBERGLASS CLOTH

This series of photographs show the basic procedures of covering a boat hull with fiberglass cloth and resin. Since the boat is sheet plywood planked, a single layer of cloth will suffice. The "dry" method (see text) is being used. The process is similar with either polyester or epoxy resin, except that if an epoxy encapsulation system is used, the surface would be coated with a thin seal coat of epoxy that would be allowed to set up first.

The fiberglass cloth is laid over the dry surface which must be clean and free of contaminants. Tape, tacks, or staples are used to hold the cloth in position on vertical surfaces. Resin is then applied in a series of "steps" or coats. The first coat bonds the cloth in place and wets it out. The second coat fills the weave of the cloth. The third coat builds up the surface sufficiently for final sanding and finishing. Note that the term "coats" may mean more than one application of resin as is explained in the text.

Note that the worker is trimming the overhanging edges of the cloth before the resin sets up hard. The fiberglass cloth yet to be applied on the hull sides will overlap the bottom cloth along the chine and other points at least several inches, providing double protection at these areas which receive abuse in use.

needed. Also, most sanding between coats is eliminated as would be required if finish resin were used throughout. Some may find this idea quite "radical", and indeed many resin suppliers will not even offer the wax additive (which is also called "surfacing agent").

The reason for this may involve the way the resin manufacturer adds the wax to the resin when he makes it. During manufacture, the resin is heated, and because of this, the paraffin wax is readily dispersed throughout the resin batch. Thus the resin manufacturer can assure a complete surface cure when the resin is used.

On the other hand, when adding your own "surfacing agent" (actually a mixture of paraffin wax held in solution by styrene, the main component of polyester resins), it is done at "room temperature" which the resin manufacturer has no control over, let alone how much is added. Thus some resin manufacturers may be leary of giving up this control over their products. However, if properly carried through, anyone can do it.

MAKING YOUR OWN POLYESTER FINISHING RESIN

For those who want to use laminating resin throughout and make their own finish resin, here's how to do it using surfacing agent. Don't attempt to "heat" the resin as manufacturers may; this is dangerous! But do try to have the resin at normal room temperature or higher, preferably around 70°F minimum. The surfacing agent should be at or above this temperature also. NOTE THAT WE'RE NOT TALKING ABOUT AIR TEMPERATURE; WE'RE TALKING ABOUT THE TEMPERATURE OF THE CONTENTS THEMSELVES.

In cold weather, the surfacing agent may appear cloudy or "filmy", or a semi-opaque solid may form on the surface of the solution in the container. If this happens, warm the container of the surfacing agent to about 90°F by placing it in a container of warm TAP water. DO NOT HEAT THE SURFACING AGENT OVER OR NEAR AN OPEN FLAME OR ELECTRIC HEATER. Also, do not allow water to enter the container. Warm the container until the solution appears clear again.

The amount of surfacing agent to use can vary between 1% and 5% BY WEIGHT OF RESIN, although 2% to 3% seems best. In other words, for each gallon of resin (which usually weighs about 9 lbs.) add approximately 2 to 4 ounces of surfacing agent, OR as noted in the instructions provided with the product. Add surfacing agent BEFORE the catalyst and stir it in well, but not so vigorously that a lot of air bubbles form in the resin. THOROUGH MIXING IS IMPORTANT! Sometimes you can see the surfacing agent in the resin as it appears as a silky "film". This filmy appearance should be well dispersed throughout the resin batch. Stir the resin frequently in use for this to occur and to assure an even cure.

If too much surfacing agent is added (a remote possibility), the resin could become too thin as the surfacing agent is partly styrene. If not enough surfacing agent is added, or not stirred in adequately, the resin surface will not cure completely; this will leave some areas with wax and other areas without. At worst the surface will have to be sanded, and this will be difficult in areas where there is no wax. Once sanded, another finish coat with more surfacing agent added will have to be applied so the previous coat will cure.

Take care when using surfacing agent as the material is harmful if inhaled or swallowed, and may irritate or damage the skin, eyes, nose, and throat. On contact, flush eyes or skin with plenty of water for at least 15 minutes. Keep it out of the reach of children, avoid breathing vapor or a spray mist, and use only with adequate ventilation. If swallowed, call a physician and induce vomiting. Keep away from flame. Keep the container closed when not in use. Wash after handling, and if any gets on your clothing, wash the clothing before re-using.

EPOXY RESIN SELECTION & HANDLING

While the epoxy resins that would be used for sheathing applications handle in much the same manner as polyesters, there are some notable distinctions and differences. As noted in Chapter 4, the resin (usually called PART "A") is mixed with a hardener (PART "B") that makes up a large portion of the mix rather than being a miniscule amount of catalyst that does not add to the amount of resin as is the case with polyesters.

Furthermore, only one epoxy resin product need be used throughout the sheathing application. There are no distinctions between "laminating" and "finishing" resin types, and in general, little or no sanding is required between coats. Epoxy resins also require no "surfacing agent" additives or other "modifications" to allow cure.

Unlike polyester resins, the epoxy types do not depend on curing by keeping air away from the surface. They cure only by the heat generated by the catalyzed mixture. This means that successive coats can be applied with little or no surface preparation between (assuming that the prior coat is smooth enough for practical purposes).

There is one qualification to the preceding that can occur with many epoxy resins. With epoxy coatings which have cured COMPLETELY (not just partially so, or which are still "tacky"), a thin, nearly invisible waxy-like film or exudite (also known as "amine blush") can occur as a by-product of curing, more or less depending on ambient conditions. This is normal. However, the film should be removed prior to applying subsequent coats or doing any sanding (it may tend to clog the paper). This is easy since the film is water soluble. Although solvents could be used, simply wipe down

the surface with a little water (some add a little ammonia, which is acceptable). The film may not occur while the resin is in a "green" or semi-cured state, and thus it is possible to keep applying subsequent coats of resin at this stage with no other prior surface preparation required.

Epoxy resins can have different curing qualities than polyesters. For example, the heat of exotherm can cause epoxy resin to become more fluid after application, making it more difficult to control runs and sags, especially if the product in use tends to have a long cure time in the first place. While a long cure time will allow plenty of working time, the worker may have to work the resin a considerable time before it sets up enough not to run or sag, especially on surfaces which are not horizontal. About the only way to speed the cure in this case is to raise surface temperatures locally, such as with heat lamps.

Although sanding between coats with epoxy resin is not an absolute necessity, a light sanding is sometimes desirable between coats. For example, after initial seal coats over the surface to be sheathed, a light sanding will knock down rough spots and raised grain which could later snag on the cloth. Or if a surface has sat overnight or longer and possibly picked up dust or other surface contamination, or has some areas of runs and sags, a little sanding is called for to clean up the surface and even it out.

PIGMENTING RESIN

Whether polyester or epoxy resin is used, a common aspect which the beginner wants advice on is pigmenting of the resin. The hope most frequently expressed is that by pigmenting the resin used in a fiberglass sheathing application, the job and expense of painting can be dispensed with. The best answer to this situation is that if you would accept a poor paint job on your car, you would probably accept the pigmented resin

a

b

c

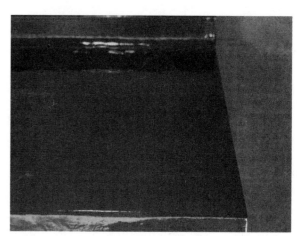

d

TEST PANEL—USING EPOXY RESIN

The techniques used to apply epoxy resin of the type used for sheathing applications are much the same as for applying polyester laminating resin. The test panel was covered with a single layer of cloth using the "dry" method and pigmented (red) epoxy resin throughout. This particular test panel was fitted with a "skeg" and inside corner fillet. The cloth has been stapled in place and the resin is being worked into the material (a).

A squeegee is being used to saturate the cloth and distribute the resin. Note that the worker is wearing protective gloves which are a "must" for epoxy, and should preferably be a butyl rubber type (unlike those shown). Too much resin was applied here to show the affects of runs and sags. Although sanding between coats is not

absolutely necessary with epoxies, the runs and sags made it necessary (b). This can slow work considerably with some epoxies since cure times may be longer than with polyesters.

A second and a third coat were applied to finish the surface after sanding (c) and (d), smoothing out the resin with a brush. The final surface was very glossy and virtually smooth enough to pass for a final finish, at least on the more-horizontal surface. However, although the pigment gave good color brilliance and depth, it was not totally opaque. The vertical surface along the skeg was less successful because of the difficulty of keeping the resin in position until it set up enough; this made sanding necessary between each coat as well as on the final coat in this area.

finish on your boat. But if you want your boat to have the look and quality of a "real yacht", attempting to pigment your resin for the purposes of omitting paint will be futile. Here's why.

While there is a place for the use of pigmented resin, which will be described shortly, the pigments available from resin suppliers are less than perfect in use. As a general rule, they are not opaque enough in the concentrations that can be mixed in the resin; you can see through them even if pigment is used in all resin coats. Unlike paints, which have a high percentage of pigment volume using high quality pigment materials, the pigments used in resin must be in a solution compatible with the resin and only so much can be added before it has a negative effect on the resin. Also, the colors ordinarily do not have the brilliance and depth of color of a good paint. Whites tend to be less than white, and dark, intense colors such as red or blue tend to fade and chalk quickly.

But the main problems with using pigments come during application, and here again part of the problem is that many novices equate the application of resin with that of paint. As noted previously, resin is NOT a paint; it applies like a poor paint. It is difficult to get a smooth, even finish, especially on vertical surfaces; resins don't level out the same as good paints. Besides, much sanding may be required on final coats as well as between coats. This sanding immediately destroys what surface gloss and color intensity may have been provided by the use of pigment, making the color appear blotchy and uneven.

To complicate the situation, resin is preferably applied in many thin coats rather than a couple of thick coatings, and attempting to mix precise amounts of pigments to yield uniform color coatings is difficult at best, no matter how carefully controlled. Besides this, pigments are not cheap, and attempting to use them throughout can raise the cost of the job

markedly. Using pigments in the resin in all coats can also make it difficult to see some types of defects such as air entrapment. In initial saturation, pigments are not advisable since they can retard saturation and make it difficult to check progress.

However, there are some reasons for, and benefits from, using pigments, at least to a limited extent, or for purposes other than final color finishes. Pigment can be added to resin as an aid in determining the evenness of the coat being applied, especially over a previously cured coat which may be unpigmented or pigmented a different contrasting color. The use of white pigment also can make it easier to spot "pinholes" which sometimes develop through coats of polyester resin. If these "pinholes" develop and are not taken care of, water may tend to enter the laminate and possibly lead to delamination.

Another benefit of using pigmented resin coats, especially when sanding will be necessary, is that it makes it easier to determine how much resin is sanded off, which is difficult to tell where you can see through to the wood using ordinary clear resin. However, only a minimal amount of pigment is necessary in this case, and uniform colored coats are not necessary.

Some people add pigment to resin in the same color that will be used for the final paint coating. This reduces or eliminates the need for a tinted undercoat or primer, plus the color will carry through to the sheathing if used in all coats, which will make surface abrasions less evident to the eye if they occur. In addition, pigments act as ultraviolet inhibitors. UV rays can cause a gradual breakdown of resin-coated surfaces, particularly those coated with epoxy.

In short, pigmenting resin is not necessary nor required for a suitable sheathing application, and will not provide a finished surface equal in appearance, quality, or durability to a well applied quality paint system. If pigmenting the resin is desired, it should be done for the benefits

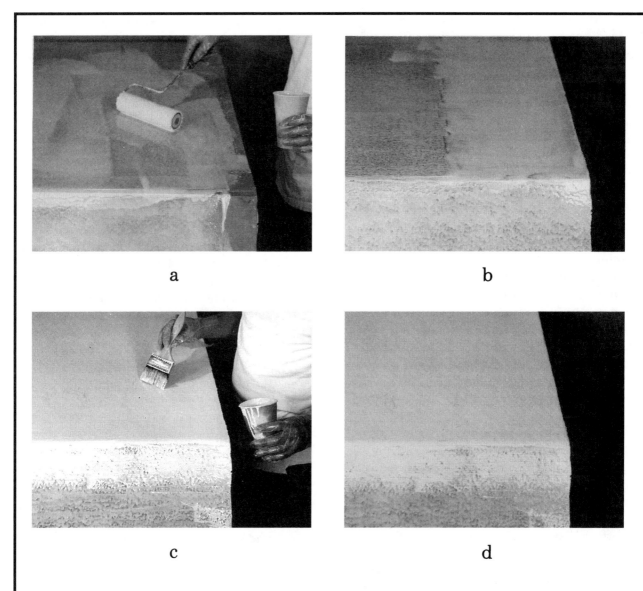

a

b

c

d

TEST PANEL—USING PIGMENTED RESIN

Using pigmented resins is usually less than successful for reasons noted in the text and as shown in these photos. A third coat of resin which has been pigmented white is being applied to the test panel previously sheathed with cloth and clear polyester resin (a). Normally this third coat would be the final coat if the resin were not pigmented. The surface would then usually be painted afterward for the final finish. However, the coat being applied now is not totally concealing the clear resin surface below. In this instance, MORE pigment was being used than recommended by the resin manufacturer, and it still did not make the surface opaque.

While a roller is normally used to apply resin in this process, the surface in this instance resulted in a stippled effect with many pock marks or craters. Part of the problem here is that a thicker

mohair paint roller is being used rather than the more preferable thin foam roller. Such surface defects can also be caused by using too much catalyst, or working when ambient temperatures are too high thereby causing the resin to "shrink" and not flow evenly due to rapid evaporation of solvents in the resin.

In (b), part of the test panel to the right was smoothed out with a brush showing the contrast with the roller. The entire resin coat was later brushed out prior to setting up, giving better results (see "c" and "d"). However, the cured surface would still require finish sanding and a paint finish coat, or at least considerable buffing and finish work for a "yachtlike" job. A more opaque surface will result if all resin coats are pigmented, but this has disadvantages also (see text).

stated above; NOT as a means to eliminate painting.

If pigments are used, make sure they are compatible with the resin used and follow the recommendations provided with the product. Do NOT add more pigment than recommended in an attempt to get a "richer" color; this can dilute the resin, and may affect the cure and physical properties adversely. Pigments are added to resin BEFORE the catalyst or hardener. With polyester resin, if using surfacing agent, this is also added before the pigment so the surfacing agent can be seen while mixing. When mixing pigments, don't be surprised if the color is affected and comes out looking different or more "murky" than you think is correct. Keep in mind that most resins impart some color in themselves, and curing also has an affect on final color.

THICKENING RESIN

As a general rule, good resins (polyester or epoxy) intended for sheathing and coating applications seldom need modification for the work at hand, and the novice should not get too "experimental" in this regard. Resin manufacturers work hard at developing products which work well over a wide range of conditions, and monkeying around with them often leads to problems.

However, there are occasions when a somewhat thicker resin would help, for example when working on a vertical or overhead surface. A thin resin can be made thicker (or more "thixotropic") by the addition of several filler materials. However, probably the most suitable such additive is fumed or colloidal silica (brand names include "Cabosil" and "Aerosil"), or "silica filler" as it is sometimes called.

The silica filler is normally added at the rate of 1% to 2% BY WEIGHT, but the stuff is so lightweight that it is impractical to measure without a very delicate scale. Thus it can be added at the rate of 5% to 10% BY VOLUME. Keep in mind that too much silica filler will prevent wetting out and saturation of the fiberglass material, and can have an adverse affect on the final qualities of the resin. Start off with small batches at first and experiment. ALWAYS wear a dust mask when working around silica filler and when stirring it in the resin.

While other filler materials may have similar affects on the resin, they may not preserve the transparent quality of the resin as does silica filler. For example, microspheres make resin opaque and give a distinct color. This type of filler also acts more like a resin extender than an agent for varying the viscosity. Thus for thickening resin, silica filler is the best choice.

THINNING AND SPRAYING RESIN

Thinning either polyester or epoxy resin should generally be avoided. The only exception is the occasional epoxy system where it is specifically called for in the initial coat (and the precise thinner is specified), or in the case of spraying of polyester resin, which will be discussed. Resin should NEVER be thinned with the idea of "stretching out" the product in the hopes of getting more coverage or saving money.

Thinners, such as acetone, do not participate in the curing process of resin and actually tend to lower the temperature of the resin, inhibiting the cure. When such solvents are sprayed, there is a tendency for them to be "trapped" in the resin, and because they can evaporate so quickly, there is a tendency to leave "pinholes" in the surface and other defects such as cracking, shrinking, and surface glazing.

A better thinner when using polyester resin is liquid styrene monomer because the resin already contains this and is compatible with it. Up to 15% of styrene can be added, but the usual proportions vary from 5% to 10%. Of course, the original viscosity of the resin in question will also have a bearing on the amount of thinning material used. Regardless, about the only reason to thin polyester resin is for spraying purposes. While some use up to 5% acetone for thinning prior to spraying, resin should NOT be thinned with acetone for any other purpose, and as just noted, even this is questionable.

Spraying of polyester resin, however, can be done and this is usually applicable to the final or finish coats. It is not practical nor necessary to spray resin for wetting out and saturating fiberglass material. A pressure-feed spray gun should be used to apply the resin as opposed to a siphon-feed type due to the viscosity of the resin. Use acetone to clean the gun BEFORE the resin sets up or else the spray gun could be ruined.

A batch of polyester resin can usually be sprayed through the gun in about 3 minutes, but the resin should be catalyzed for a pot life of from 15 to 20 minutes. If flaws or thick areas build up, use a brush or roller to smooth out these areas before the resin gels. The technique is otherwise the same as spraying paint so that anyone familiar with paint spraying should have no problem adapting to polyester resin. The hazards are also similar to volatile paint systems.

Repeated coats of resin can be sprayed on as long as the surface does not set up. If a delay occurs or the resin does set up, the surface should be sanded before spraying additional coats when using finish resin. Spraying resin puts a lot of fumes and spray mist into the air which can be dangerous. Use only with adequate ventilation, wear a respirator, and avoid any open flames, heat sources, or smoking in the area. Do NOT attempt to spray in direct sunlight or in a windy or drafty area.

Spraying of epoxy resin is simply not done for sheathing and coating applications. The reasons are simple. Epoxy systems are usually "100% solids" formulations; that is, the products in the resin and

hardener cure to form a solid plastic with no by-products resulting and no other products necessary for cure to occur. In fact, adding other chemicals such as thinners may have an adverse or even destructive affect. Without the addition of thinners, epoxy resins usually are of such a viscosity that it is impractical for them to pass through spray equipment, not to mention the added hazards that could occur and the cost of material wasted in potential overspray. Proper clean-up of equipment using epoxy resin is difficult, tedious, and costly, and if epoxy sets up in your spray equipment, it will be ruined.

MIXING RESIN WITH CATALYST OR HARDENER

Catalyst added to polyester resin, and hardener added to epoxy resin, should be measured carefully, following the manufacturer's directions regarding proportions. While variations in catalyst are common with polyester resins to suit ambient conditions, this is seldom the case with epoxies. Thus with polyester resins, it may take one or two batches of resin before the proper working time in relation to ambient temperatures is arrived at. This is why it is recommended to start out with a small area, such as the transom of a boat, when doing a big job. With epoxy resins, NEVER attempt to vary the hardener proportion in an attempt to vary the pot life.

With polyester resin that may be old, MORE catalyst may also be required, OR perhaps LESS. This seeming contradiction depends on the resin formulation and whether or not the styrene has evaporated from the resin. If the styrene has NOT evaporated, LESS catalyst will be required as the resin will be nearer to curing due to its age. However, there is no practical way to tell if the styrene has evaporated and thus the only way to find out the cure qualities of an old resin is to try a batch and wait. Fresh resin is therefore preferable.

When mixing in the catalyst or hardener, ALWAYS use a fresh stirring stick for EACH batch. NEVER use a stick from a previous batch which may have partially cured resin on it; this may cause an uneven or premature cure, or affect the pot life. Stirring sticks should be clean bare wood that you buy or make yourself. CAREFUL STIRRING IS IMPORTANT! Stir by hand, but NOT vigorously. Take care to scrape all surfaces of the mixing container (sides and bottom) for at least a minute and preferably more, particularly with epoxies. Then apply the batch immediately.

The use of power mixers, such as those attachments which can be used with electric drills, are not recommended. These can be dangerous and they cause air to become entrapped in the resin, sometimes leading to frothing. It is also difficult to adequately scrape the container sides and bottom with such attachments, and they actually are more difficult to use since they require proper cleaning after each use.

COMPATIBILITY OF POLYESTER & EPOXY RESINS

Many amateur boatbuilders are confused about whether epoxy resin can be used over polyester resin and vice versa. As noted in Chapter 4, the resins should NEVER be mixed while BOTH are in the wet, uncured state. This means don't apply a coat of one type over a wet or uncured coating of the other type. However, once one is cured, the other uncured resin will have no affect on it. Wet epoxy resin will not "attack" cured polyester, and wet polyester will not "attack" cured epoxy. In other words, they are "compatible" in this sense.

Practical aspects of this situation arise commonly in boatbuilding. For example, a wood boat may be assembled with epoxy glues, or fastening holes may be filled with epoxy filler. If the owner wants to sheathe such a boat with fiberglass, should epoxy or polyester be used?

A basic premise is that epoxy resin will stick to just about anything, including cured surfaces coated with polyester resin. However, polyester resins don't stick quite as well to cured epoxy surfaces. Does this mean that polyester resin cannot be used over a bare wood surface with epoxy glue lines and filled areas? No, because a MAJORITY of the area is still bare wood; the epoxied joints and fastening holes are inconsequential in area and thus will not cause any major loss of bond of the sheathing at areas of contact with cured epoxy.

However, had the ENTIRE surface been coated with epoxy and allowed to cure, then a polyester coating applied over this would be a poor choice; it would not stick well. Similarly, applying an epoxy coating over a cured polyester coating, while it would bond, would not make much sense. The bonding ability of the epoxy would only be as good as that of the polyester substrate.

BASIC RESIN APPLICATION PROCEDURES

The following gives a general scenario of what takes place once the resin has been mixed with catalyst or hardener and is ready for application. Specific application procedures used with various sheathing materials and combinations are described later. The following information thus serves as sort of an "introduction" of how to work with the resin side of the equation and what to expect.

Once the resin has been mixed with catalyst or hardener (and perhaps some other additives as the case may be), don't worry about daubing the resin on as might be done with paint. Instead, promptly pour the resin on the surface (not necessarily the entire batch, however) and use the applications tools to spread it around. A squeegee is probably the best tool to move a lot of resin around initially.

This is not the time to linger; you'll probably need all the time you can get to make a good application of the resin batch before it starts to gel. Once the resin does start to get like "jelly", or it starts forming "threads" or otherwise becomes "sticky" and "stringy", STOP APPLICATION IMMEDIATELY! Make no further attempt to apply more resin from this batch. Don't try to mix up another batch of resin in this container or stir a new batch with the same stick used in the preceding. Throw away the remaining resin along with the stirring stick used.

If there is quite a lot of resin remaining after gelation starts, pour it out onto the ground somewhere where it can be well dispersed and not concentrated, and in such a manner so that it can be picked up and disposed of properly after it sets up. The reason for this is that once curing begins, considerable heat may be generated (perhaps enough to burn combustibles), and this is why it should NOT be deposited in containers of refuse.

Once the resin starts to gel, wait until the surface has reached a firm gel or has at least become "tacky" before making another application of resin over it. With polyester resin, the more experienced worker can, however, "catch" a gelled area with a fresh batch of resin and retard gelation somewhat if additional work on the area is required. This is a somewhat tricky procedure and should only be attempted after some experience is gained.

Up to the point that the resin begins to gel, you should have worked the resin as long as possible with the application tools (such as rollers and squeegees) to prevent and eliminate runs and sags, particularly on surfaces that are other than horizontal. If there is seemingly more resin than is required (it will be evident from a tendency to run and sag), the excess should be removed from the surface and discarded.

A MOST IMPORTANT POINT: THE MOST COMMON MISTAKE FOR THE NOVICE WHICH CAUSES EXCESS WORK LATER IS USING TOO MUCH RESIN. Use only as much resin in each coat as is necessary to do the job, whether you are wetting out the fiberglass or are simply applying a coating. It is FAR better to apply MORE coats which are thinner than it is to attempt to lay on less coats which are heavier; sags and runs will be inevitable with this latter practice. The sanding and grinding then required to get a smooth, even finish once the resin sets up will prove tedious and frustrating.

This is not to imply, however, that some sanding and finish work will not be required. Such is NOT the case. However, if you take care in the resin application, using only as much resin as is required and keep coats thin and free of runs and sags, this will go a long way towards keeping such work limited.

Most sheathing applications go much faster than the typical beginner imagines. Small boats can often be completed up to the finishing stage in a day or so, and even the largest boats can be done in a matter of days. This should not be misconstrued that you can't take longer, although long periods should not be allowed to transpire between coats, especially with polyester resins. Long time spans between coatings set up so-called "secondary bonding" conditions, which in polyester resin is never as sound as the "primary" bond that occurs between resin coats which are essentially "green" or not fully cured yet.

Thus if a day or more transpires between resin coats (that is, a coat of resin essentially cures prior to a subsequent coat), prudent practice is to at least lightly sand the surface and/or give a solvent wash so that any surface contamination will not occur and affect the bond of the next coat.

How long should you wait before you put your newly fiberglassed boat in the water? This varies depending on ambient temperatures, humidity, and any of those things which affect cure times. With polyester resins WAIT AT LEAST 48 HOURS; three days OR MORE is even better. With epoxy resin, WAIT AT LEAST 7 DAYS. In the meantime, with either polyester or epoxy resin, don't expose the fiberglass job to rainy weather, fog, dew, or direct sunlight.

SHEATHING APPLICATIONS USING FIBERGLASS MATERIALS

The several common fiberglass materials available (i.e., cloth, mat, and woven roving) make possible several potential combinations in a sheathing application. For example, an all-cloth covering might be used, or one including a layer each of mat and cloth, or another consisting of mat and woven roving. This section will explore the merits of some of these various combinations.

Most boat sheathing applications are basic and simple, involving the use of fiberglass cloth. Usually a single or a double layer of fiberglass cloth will suffice. While more layers of cloth can be used, cost becomes a factor, and a point begins to be reached where the sheathing begins to assume much more of a structural role than is necessary or practical.

To diverge for a moment, this brings up a topic which comes up frequently, especially with builders of sheet plywood boats. Many amateur builders come up with the idea of reducing the thickness of the plywood and making up the thickness with a build-up of fiberglass materials and resin. The "reasoning" behind this idea is based on some myths and fallacies regarding fiberglass, and generally should not be done.

First, the novice has been led to believe that by using more fiberglass instead of plywood, his boat will not only be lighter in weight, but stronger as well. The fact is,

it just ain't so! For a given thickness, plywood is ALWAYS much lighter in weight. If you don't believe this, take a one-foot-square piece of plywood in any thickness, then lay up a similar sized slab of fiberglass (you can use mat, cloth, woven roving, or any combination) to the same thickness. Next, take both samples and throw them in the pond; which one floats? The plywood sample! The fiberglass sample quickly goes to the bottom because it's heavier. Furthermore, if the same two samples are put on edge, the plywood panel will be obviously stiffer.

Thus if you reduce the thickness of plywood planking, even with an addition of fiberglass in an attempt to make up for it, you will lose stiffness in the hull while at the same time increase the weight (not to mention the cost). Such a practice just adds to the difficulty of getting a good finish. Again the point should be emphasized that a fiberglass sheathing is NOT provided for additional strength in a well-designed, well-built plywood boat.

The majority of sheet plywood boats and those of similar stable wood planking suffice with a sheathing application using one layer of cloth. A second layer can be used where conditions of use might be beyond those to which a pleasure boat is subjected.

However, in such cases with two layers of cloth, epoxy resin is preferable. The reason is that the bond between successive layers of cloth with polyester resin (also referred to as "peel strength") is not as good as it should be; epoxy is superior in this regard. Thus, in polyester applications where more protection is necessary than that offered by a single layer of cloth, a layer of mat should first be used against the hull with this overlaid with a layer of cloth. Interlaminar bond or "peel strength" between the mat and cloth is much improved, and the mat forms a better bond to the wood than does the cloth when using polyester resin. Remember that epoxy resin

SHEATHING A SMALL DINGHY WITH FIBERGLASS CLOTH & RESIN

This series of photos show the various operations applicable in sheathing applications using cloth on just about any sized boat. Screw holes and other minor imperfections are filled with a hard-setting putty and sanded smooth as in (a) and (b). The bottom cloth is fitted slightly oversize; note the overlaps at the corners as shown in (c). In this small boat the bottom cloth also covers each end in one piece because of the simple hull shape.

The cloth is wetted out with resin using the "dry method" as in (d) with overhanging edges trimmed off just before the resin sets

up hard as in (e). Edges at overlapping areas are feathered as is being done in (f) and then the side covering is fitted as in (g) and wetted out beginning at the top as in (h). Note the masking tape used to hold the cloth. Additional resin is applied with a thin foam roller to complete wetting out the cloth as in (i). At this point, the resin will keep the cloth in place and the masking tape removed as in (j). A small boat such as this can usually be completed in a matter of hours up to the point of doing finish work.

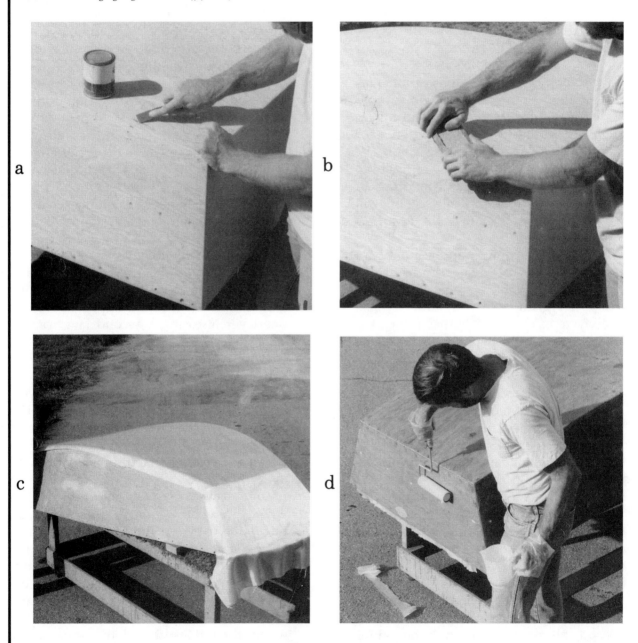

a

b

c

d

e

f

g

h

i

j

should not usually be used with mat.

Occasionally a sheathing application may be required where even greater protection than offered by cloth, or mat and cloth, is necessary, such as workboats where appearance and weight are not critical. In these cases, woven roving and mat can be used together with polyester resins. The mat is again used against the surface with the woven roving applied over this. Don't attempt to use only woven roving in two or more layers; the "peel strength" and bond strength to the hull in this combination are poor. Also, epoxy resin should not be used either.

TWO BASIC TECHNIQUES FOR SHEATHING APPLICATIONS

There are basically two techniques used in applying sheathings with fiberglass cloth. One technique is referred to as the "WET METHOD" and the other is called the "DRY METHOD". The "wet method" refers to the laying of the cloth onto a wet catalyzed resin surface, smoothing it out, saturating it, and then applying subsequent coats of resin.

The "dry method" refers to laying the cloth on a bare uncoated or "dry" surface (or on one which may have been coated with resin that has been allowed to set up hard), and then soaking and forcing catalyzed resin through the cloth, thereby saturating both the cloth and the bonding surface. Subsequent coats are later applied just as with the "wet method". In either method, the end results should be identical.

When reading literature concerning fiberglassing, particularly dated, unenlightened material, you may find instructions to the effect that "the surface should be coated with resin FIRST, then allowed to set up slightly, and then the cloth applied"—this pretty well describes the "wet method". For reasons which will become obvious, the "wet method" is usually a waste of time,

more work, tedious, and messy. Although there is nothing basically wrong with the "wet method", there is a technical situation when using polyester resin that can lead to potential poor bonding conditions, and it's the author's opinion that this has led to delamination problems in the past.

One of the reasons often heard for using the "wet method" is that some woods tend to absorb resin at an unequal rate; that is, the resin soaks into the wood in one area but not in another. The reasoning behind the "wet method" is to allow the worker to apply an even coat of resin by going over areas where this occurs.

However, the fallacy is that this same effect occurs even when a layer of cloth is applied over the bare surface first and is then saturated with resin as in the "dry method". The areas where the resin tends to soak into the wood show up equally well with the cloth in position, and hence additional resin can still be applied just as easily to any dry areas. Also, in practical applications, especially with Douglas fir plywood, there does not seem to be much of a problem in extremes between areas of a surface where the wood tends to soak up resin and other areas which remain "wet" with resin.

There may be some justification for using the "wet method" on vertical or overhead surfaces where the tacky resin may seem better able to hold the cloth in position. However, in most instances, there will be an opportunity to tack or staple the cloth to hold it in position, and if not, it would be preferable to get more helpers to hold the cloth in place while another worker uses the neater, easier "dry method" to wet out the cloth.

For the inexperienced amateur, the "wet method" adds the potential for a further problem that can be the precursor for future delamination when using polyester resin. The success of the "wet method" depends on laying the cloth into wet resin. However, the pot life of resin is only about 15 or 20 minutes at best, and may be less in hot weather. Thus it's possible that the cloth may not get wetted out completely, and stretched in place with all wrinkles removed. If this occurs, a potential secondary bonding situation is set up which may lead to a questionable bond of the sheathing to the surface; this cannot occur with the dry method.

USING THE "WET METHOD"

There may come a time when the "wet method" may be desired, and here's how to do it. First, lay the cloth on the area to be covered and cut roughly to shape. For large areas it may not be necessary to do this as the material can be unrolled directly onto the surface. In any case, leave plenty of cloth at the edges, joints, and any overlaps, say 4" to 6". Roll the cloth onto a mailing tube, dowel, broom stick, or other similar cylinder, and set aside where it won't get soiled but will be immediately available.

Next apply the resin. Only a limited area can be coated before gelation occurs, and of course the cloth must be applied BEFORE the resin starts to set up. You'll have to work fast. This means that only so much cloth can be unrolled onto the resin-coated surface at a time. The cloth should be cut where the resin coat stops unless the work can be done fast enough to continue applying resin before gelation forces a stop. If the cloth is cut too late (after the resin starts to set), there will be a protruding area which will have to be feathered out for the next adjoining piece. If the cloth is not cut, resin MUST be applied continuously along the length of the cloth to prevent any premature gelation.

For most beginners working alone, it is best to limit the area worked to about 20 to 30 square feet at a time, cut the cloth, and make a joint with the next piece. Of course, on an area such as the transom of a boat, a joint would probably not be required so there would be no problem in this regard.

Therefore, you might want to try the wet method in such an area to see how you like it. As can be seen, however, on large surfaces, many joints along the length of the cloth could be required. But with the "dry method" to be described, no joints would be necessary.

If using the "wet method" with polyester resin, use ONLY laminating resin. The reason is that in applying the initial coat, it would be next to impossible to remove the wax which would float to the surface if using finish resin, especially if the work could not be done fast enough to get a second coat of resin applied. The wax would then get into the weave of the fiberglass cloth, and if the resin did set up, the cloth would not be totally covered with resin. If such resin were allowed to cure, a poor bond for subsequent coats would result.

Since the only way to remove all the wax after this time would be to sand, it would be virtually impossible to avoid sanding through much of the cloth, thereby ruining the sheathing. Thus, if a resin with wax IS used, the buildup of resin on the cloth must be adequate first before sanding to prevent sanding through the cloth; this is difficult to do. For this reason, if you are using finishing resin throughout, it is better to use the "dry method" described later.

When using laminating resin with the "wet method", sanding the surface with the fiberglass cloth partly exposed is not necessary. Once the laminating resin starts to gel and cure, additional coats can be applied without further ado.

As might be deduced from the above, one of the problems with the "wet method" can be getting good saturation of the cloth with the first and second coats of resin. Part of the reason for this is the fact that the resin cannot be applied to the entire area at precisely the same time before applying the cloth, and some resin may start to cure or gel while some of it will still be wet. The resin which is fairly wet will saturate the cloth well, but that resin which has been on

TEST PANEL—APPLYING FIBERGLASS CLOTH WITH THE "WET" METHOD

The test panel simulates a typical hull section including a "skeg" (a) that is to be covered with a single layer of fiberglass cloth and resin using the "wet" method. A wood cant strip has been installed along the inside corner prior to applying the cloth so the cloth will adhere to this area (d). The cloth has been previously fitted to the area and rolled onto a cardboard tube.

The side of the test panel has been protected with paper and masking tape to prevent any resin from running and curing onto the side. A coat of resin is applied to the bare surface and while still wet, the roll of fiberglass cloth is unrolled onto the surface (b). Getting the cloth unrolled into the same position when it was first cut can be tricky because it can't be moved around too much without forming wrinkles and air bubbles.

The cloth is smoothed out and saturated as much as possible with the first coat. The photo (b) shows parts of the cloth where the first coat of resin is saturating through from the back side. A second coat of resin is applied immediately after the cloth is in position and smoothed out (c).

The panel has been sanded after the third coat of resin (d). The dark spots indicate low areas which means another coat of resin will be required to build these up (four coats total). Note the cant strip at the inside corner. The side is being covered after completing the bottom (e), although the sequence on an actual boat makes little difference. The resin initially applied to the surface is forced through the cloth with a squeegee. The "dry" or white areas will require more resin.

the surface longer can make it difficult to wet out the cloth. One thing that may help in this regard is to UNDER-catalyze the resin somewhat (if working with polyester) so more time is available to wet out the cloth. Getting the cloth saturated is a "must", and under no circumstances should you wait to apply the cloth AFTER gelation begins; a bond may not result.

When applying the first coat of catalyzed resin, quickly spread the resin around with a squeegee, then use a brush or roller to even out the coating, but lay on a good full-bodied coat. A roller works faster and can be used to quickly spread resin in all directions. If it appears that the resin is soaking into the wood, apply more resin over these areas. A dry area will appear dull so it is easy to spot. The cloth should be applied immediately after. However, if the resin is allowed to "stiffen up" a bit first, the cloth will not slip and move around on resin that is too wet. In other words, the cloth must be applied at just the right point if the job is to be made easier.

Take the cloth rolled onto the cylinder and start unrolling it by hand over the surface to position it and work in the resin. This is pretty messy work and is not required with the "dry method". Sometimes it is difficult to get the cloth in the same position it was when fitted, and this can be hectic. Also, there is a tendency for sticky hands to drag and move the cloth about. Use a squeegee to work out wrinkles and air bubbles, and pull the cloth along edges to fit. Try to do the saturation as quickly and completely as possible so that another coat can be applied if at all possible to conceal the weave of the cloth. There must be no white or "milky" areas where the weave of the cloth appears. When totally saturated and wetted out, the weave will disappear and be transparent.

The foregoing describes the basic initial procedures of the "wet method". The balance of this chapter beyond the description of the "dry method" should be read for in-

formation in completing the job, including various application "tips" that will allow a proper finished application.

USING THE "DRY METHOD"

With the 'dry method', the fiberglass cloth is spread over a dry surface initially. This can be the bare wood surface of the hull, or in the case of boats incorporating wood epoxy encapsulating systems, a seal coat of epoxy is applied to the wood first and allowed to cure. A light sanding is usually recommended after this to take care of any snags or raised grain areas that might interfere with the cloth application. Whatever the case, the underlying surface is dry.

The cloth can be cut to shape, but this is not necessary as it can be done later. The cloth can be tacked, stapled, or even taped in position with masking tape (remove tacks or staples just prior to the resin setting up). However, note that resin will tend to dissolve the adhesive used in masking tape, but by the time it does, the cloth will usually be secure enough in position by virtue of the resin (except on vertical surfaces where it could slip). If polyester resin is used, the resin can be laminating resin (wax free) for the initial coats. However, finish resin (containing wax) can be used throughout, albeit with the difficulties between coats previously described.

Pour the resin promptly onto the surface directly from the container wherever possible to save time. As with the "wet method", an area of approximately 30 square feet can usually be worked by one person before the resin starts to gel. However, as long as the application is continuous, there is no need to worry about cutting the cloth and making joints. All that is required is to mix up a fresh batch of resin and proceed along the length of the cloth into the next area.

The resin is then forced through the cloth preferably using a squeegee or roller, with a brush being used in certain hard-to-reach areas such as inside corners. Otherwise a brush is usually too slow, although some have had luck using a large stiff-bristled brush such as those used to apply wallpaper. Rollers spread resin around quickly, and the squeegee smooths out the cloth and can be used to scrape off any excess resin. Take care in using the squeegee, however, as it can tend to pull the cloth out of position if worked too vigorously.

With the "dry method" there is usually no problem in saturating the cloth or in building up the resin evenly in the cloth. In working the resin through the cloth, the cloth acts as a screed that assures a uniform minimum thickness coating. However, as is typical with the uninformed beginner, do NOT use TOO MUCH resin at this point, especially on vertical or inclined surfaces. Use only enough resin to bond and wet out the cloth; the weave of the cloth can be built up later with successive coats. If runs and sags appear, work the resin longer and get rid of excess resin.

Another common problem is that the cloth will not adhere well around outside or inside corners, usually because they have not been radiused sufficiently. The resin tends to "bleed out" as the cloth lifts. If this occurs, keep working the resin into these areas until it begins to set up. If an area is stubborn and does not receive adequate saturation, it is possible to cut out the cloth with a razor knife before the resin sets up completely and apply a patch of new cloth and resin.

If the resin does set up and an area does contain bubbles where the cloth has lifted, the cloth must be sanded through and the adjoining edges must be feathered so a patch of fresh cloth can be inserted. Such a patch should overlap onto sound cloth some distance for integrity of the sheathing. To minimize or prevent these problems, be sure that any corners are well radiused FIRST and the surface prepared properly. The balance of the chapter gives information for completing the job, including vari-

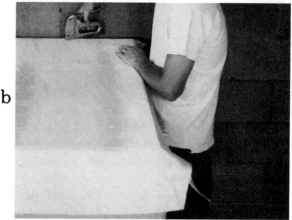

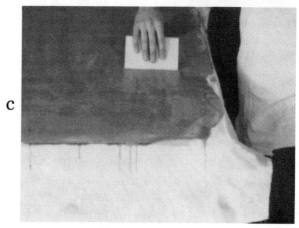

TEST PANEL—APPLYING FIBERGLASS CLOTH WITH THE "DRY" METHOD

The side of the test panel is masked with paper just below the point where the bottom cloth will lap onto the side (a). The fiberglass cloth is fitted to rough oversize over the bare dry surface and stapled in place (b). A coat of resin is poured onto the cloth surface and distributed with a squeegee or roller (c). Polyester

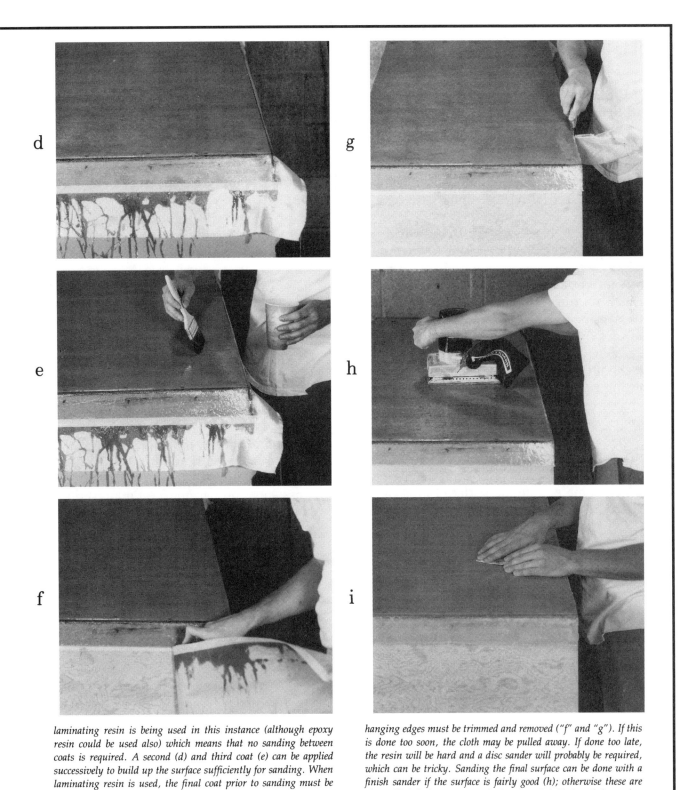

laminating resin is being used in this instance (although epoxy resin could be used also) which means that no sanding between coats is required. A second (d) and third coat (e) can be applied successively to build up the surface sufficiently for sanding. When laminating resin is used, the final coat prior to sanding must be mixed with surfacing agent so the resin will set up tack-free. Alternately, a finishing resin containing wax could be used.

Before the resin sets up hard, the masked area as well as over-hanging edges must be trimmed and removed ("f" and "g"). If this is done too soon, the cloth may be pulled away. If done too late, the resin will be hard and a disc sander will probably be required, which can be tricky. Sanding the final surface can be done with a finish sander if the surface is fairly good (h); otherwise these are slow. Slightly low areas can be hand sanded (i), but if the surface is very irregular, another coat of resin may be required. Other approaches to finishing are given in the text.

ous application situations that are usually confronted in any sheathing application.

SUMMARY OF BASIC STEPS IN THE SHEATHING APPLICATION

The "wet method" and the "dry method" are the two basic methods used for applying sheathing materials. Either method can be used on vertical or horizontal surfaces, and though seldom required, many prefer the "wet method" when working overhead, especially if labor is short. The following summarizes the basic steps as described in the text. Variations may be required depending on the resin type used (e.g. laminating resin, finish resin, epoxy, etc.), degree of surface quality desired, tools and equipment used, and other factors. The text should be read thoroughly before commencing the sheathing application in order to fully understand the various factors involved.

"WET METHOD"

1. Fit the material to the surface to rough size.
2. Roll the material onto a cylinder tube or dowel and set aside.
3. Coat the surface with a full coating of mixed resin.
4. Unroll the material onto the wet surface, smoothing out wrinkles and air bubbles.
5. Apply another coat of resin over the cloth to saturate it.
6. Apply additional coats of resin to fill the weave of the cloth and provide a sanding base.

"DRY METHOD"

1. Fit the material to the surface to rough size and tack, staple, or tape in position.

2. Saturate the cloth covered surface with mixed resin.
3. Smooth out wrinkles and air bubbles before the resin sets up.
4. Apply additional coats of resin to fill the weave of the cloth and provide a sanding base.

CONTINUOUS VERSUS STOP-&-GO OPERATION

In the descriptions of both the "wet method" and the "dry method" it is presumed that one worker is doing the job. In these cases, it is ordinary to do a section or area, allow the resin to set up at least partially, do whatever is necessary in preparation for the next coat (such as feather seams, knock down any rough spots, etc.), apply subsequent coats, and move along to the next area. In other words, there will be times when a worker will be waiting, and to some this is a waste of time.

However, as experience is gained, or if two or more workers are available, some techniques can be used so that the fiberglass sheathing application may be done in one continuous operation along a given length of cloth. For example, with the "wet method", one worker can apply resin while another rolls on the length of cloth progressively, wets it out, and smooths it in place after, all without the need to make any joints. This works fine as long as the batches of resin can be continuously mixed and applied without let-up and everyone is well organized.

The same principle applies to the "dry method", although the cloth will already be in place. The secret here is to start at one end applying resin, and progressively wetting out the cloth from a wet to a dry area. Immediately following the cloth application, another worker can be laying on the second, and even final, coats as long as laminating resin is being used and previous coats are allowed to set up somewhat first.

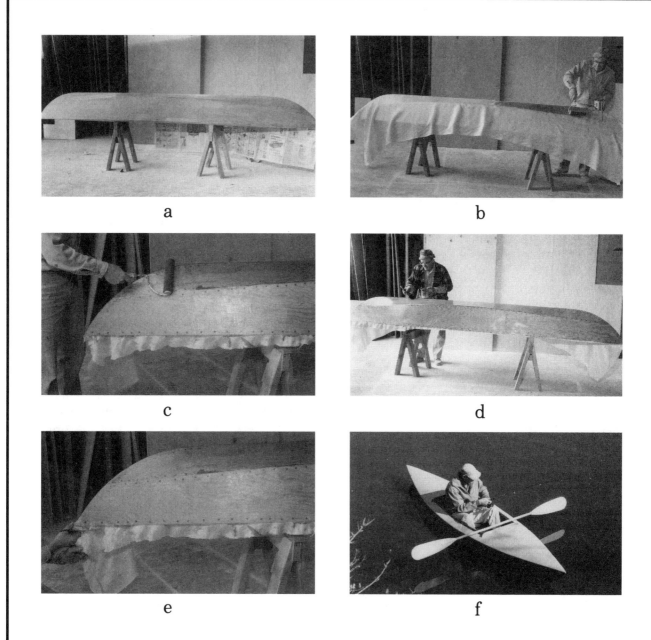

a

b

c

d

e

f

COVERING SMALL BOATS WITH FIBERGLASS CLOTH & RESIN

Sometimes it is possible to cover a small boat with a single piece of fiberglass cloth with no joints or overlaps as is being done in this group of photographs. The bare hull has been prepared to receive the cloth with all screw holes and minor imperfections filled with a compatible wood putty (a). All corners have been gently radiused so the cloth will conform to the hull without forming air bubbles.

The length of cloth is draped over the hull and the resin applied in a continuous operation for each coat (b). A roller is used to distribute the resin quickly, while a brush is used in areas where required (c) and (d). Overhanging edges of the cloth are trimmed

before the resin sets up hard (e).

On this boat, the fiberglass cloth overhanging along the gunwhale was trimmed flush with the deck surface and the deck was covered later overlapping onto the sides. However, the fiberglass cloth could have been trimmed up to the deck edge and then capped with a rub rail without covering the deck surface. When using one piece of cloth as is done here, no overlaps or joints are required in the cloth. The completed craft is protected from leaks, has a neat appearance, and will not require any maintenance for many seasons (f).

This whole procedure is much like the painting principle of keeping and working into a "wet edge".

The key word, however, is CONTINUOUS application, for as soon as the work along a piece of cloth is halted (for example, time runs out or the resin begins to gel), a joint would be required. In other words, if a length of cloth cannot be applied in a normal work period, for example one day, a joint must be made in order to recommence the application on another day. This should not be confused with a lap or butt joint that might occur with parallel pieces of cloth which can be applied at any later period without problems using either the "wet method" or "dry method". These statements apply only along the length of a given piece of cloth where it is necessary to make a stop; the next adjoining piece may be either lapped or butted as required.

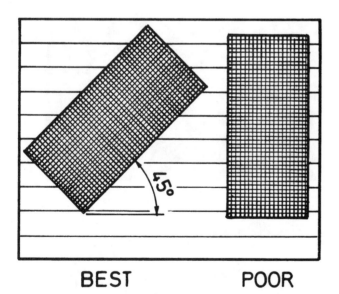

BEST   POOR

When applying any cloth or woven material over a planked surface, greater strength will result if the material is applied at an approximate 45° angle to the planking seams. This will orient strands in two directions. If the material is applied in line or at right angles to the seams, only the strands crossing the seams will be providing strength; the strands parallel to the seams will make no strength contribution.

HOW MANY COATS ARE REQUIRED IN A SHEATHING APPLICATION?

Basically, a sheathing application is nominally considered a four-coat process if the "wet method" is used, and a three-coat process if the "dry method" is used. However, this is not to be taken precisely, as will be pointed out. It is NOT the number of coats that is important. What IS important is that sufficient resin must be applied to wet out the cloth, fill the weave, and build up a resin coating that is thick enough to permit sanding without cutting into the sheathing material, yet thin enough to keep weight down and prevent too brittle a coating.

In the "wet method", the first wet coat may be considered a "seal" or "bedding" coat; the resin coats or "seals" the surface and the material is bedded in it. The next coat in the "wet method" and the first coat in the "dry method" can be called a "bonding" or "saturating" coat. This coat bonds the material to the surface and wets out the fiberglass. In the "dry method", this coat also performs the function of the first coat used in the "wet method". The next coat in either method is a "fill" coat; it builds up resin and fills the weave of the cloth. The final coat is the "finish" or "sanding" coat; much of this coat is usually sanded away to smooth out the surface in preparation for painting.

The use of thin foam rollers has been somewhat of a revolutionary advancement in resin coat application. In the past, it was more difficult to build up uniform thickness coats of resin after initial coats were applied by squeegee, especially with heavy-napped mohair rollers or those made of thicker foams. The tendency of these rollers was to retain copious amounts of resin, thereby making coatings too thick, which led to runs and sags and tedious sanding, even though the prescribed three or four coats applied were more than sufficient for a proper application.

However, the thin foam rollers now available give much better control of coating thickness and quality even though more coats may be required to obtain optimum coating thickness. In other words, the same amount of resin may eventually be deposited on the surface as with older methods, but more coats (especially fill and finish coats) may be required to do so. Thus, the three or four coat procedure now really describes the actual "steps" required for application rather than being a literal count of the actual coats that may be required.

To the novice, applying more coats may seem like more work, but this is not true. Rolling on resin with thin foam rollers is quick and easy once the cloth has been applied and wetted out. It may take a bit longer rolling out the coats, but the control of runs and sags and surface quality, and the resulting sanding effort saved, is more than worth it.

SANDING BETWEEN COATS

If polyester finishing resin is used for the application, each coat that sets up must be sanded to remove the wax which raises to the surface. While it would seem that this wax could be removed with a solvent wipe, when this is attempted, it just tends to shove the wax around to a different spot; it does not come off completely. Thus sanding is the only suitable method.

If using polyester laminating resin or epoxy resin, and smooth, even coats are applied, there is technically no need to do any sanding between coats assuming that no dirt, dust, grease, or other contaminants get on the surface which could affect the bond of future coats, and not too long a period of time transpires between coats (no more than a day or so). However, with epoxy resins, if a thin, wax-like film (amine blush) develops after cure, this should be wiped off with plain water prior to applying the next coat, and before any sanding is done.

If a coated surface has some nubs, raised wood grain, rough spots, high areas, runs, or sags, these should be knocked down or smoothed out prior to applying the next coat. In these cases, sanding will be easiest if it is done within a day, since the longer the resin sets, the harder it gets (up to a point of total cure). In fact, there is a point in the cure cycle of polyester resin where it is easiest to sand; this point is not too long after the resin is just tack-free, but still in a "green" state.

If sanding is to be done on cured polyester laminating resin, it will prove difficult as the paper will tend to clog quickly. In this instance, some prefer to lay on what is best called a "hot coat"; this is a thin, somewhat over-catalyzed coat of finishing resin which will make such sanding easier. This can also be done over limited areas where sanding will be required, such as lap joints where feathering will be required. Also, a solvent wipe prior to sanding tends to make the sanding easier in all cases.

Throughout the application of resin, attempt to lay on coats that are thin and even so that sanding can be minimized. Remember that the quality of each coat will be magnified through to the final surface and any underlying defects will be "telegraphed" to the surface where they will be readily apparent and perhaps of greater magnitude than they seemed earlier.

A disc sander is perfect for feathering edges at corners and joints, although care must be taken not to gouge into any adjacent bare wood area. A foam pad attachment will minimize this tendency. A belt sander can be used over broader areas if used with care. A finish sander will smooth out a surface well, but these are slow and will not remove much material. Hand sanding will be required in those areas where machine sanders can't reach.

In attempting to even out a surface, low spots tend to show up "glossy", whereas sanded areas will have a "frosted" or matte finish. Be careful if using a machine sander at corners as it is easy to go through the material. Hand sanding of corners is often better since this is one spot where an extra buildup of material is preferable. Remove any sanding dust from the surface prior to applying additional coats.

WORKING ON VERTICAL SURFACES

Most people have good luck using resin on fairly flat surfaces. But vertical surfaces can often be disheartening. One reason for this is that some people put too much faith in resins which are advertised as "thixotropic—won't run or sag". They then proceed to use such resins fully convinced that they will apply like a good paint and not run or sag, only to find out that this is not what indeed occurs.

While it is true that there are resins which will run and sag MORE than others, it is best to proceed with the thought that ALL resins will run, and then take preventative action to stop or at least minimize running and sagging.

One way to prevent sags and runs is to use LESS resin and make good use of the squeegee at the same time. Beginners often attempt to apply too much resin, and if there is more resin on the surface than the fiberglass material can absorb, or more than a coating can tolerate, sheer gravity will make it run down no matter how "thixotropic" the resin may be. Thus use MINIMUM amounts of resin to prevent this; you can always add more.

On vertical surfaces, because the resin will run, work the area in all directions as long as possible until the resin begins to gel. Use foam rollers once the cloth is wetted out. If the resin is running out or leaching out from an upper area, use a squeegee to move the resin back up into this area again. If using polyester resin, putting a bit more catalyst in the resin initially will make it set up faster and reduce the time such work is necessary before the resin starts to gel.

Many people think that they can use a brush on vertical surfaces and "paint" or even out a coat of resin much as they would with a good enamel. But resin does not work this way, especially on vertical surfaces. Using a brush working in one direction first appears to even out the resin, but shortly after, the resin begins to show runs and sags again, in addition to often showing pockmarks or craters or an overly stippled surface.

If the brush strokes are in a horizontal direction along the vertical surface, the sags appear in a prominent horizontal line. Better luck comes by using brush strokes in a vertical direction, but even still, the surface problem recurs. The problem is that the brush (whose purpose is to provide an even but consistently thick coat of paint) distributes the resin, but does not get rid of excess resin; this is what a squeegee is for, and rollers should be used in place of the brush.

EDGES, CORNERS, JOINTS, & OVERLAPS

The manner of handling joints in sheathing applications varies, and some debate exists on how to approach them. Because of the high bonding capabilities of epoxy resins and their lack of shrinkage, joints between sections of cloth (whether along edges or at ends) are commonly NOT overlapped; such joints can simply be butted. Some may argue that this results in a loss of continuity in strength of the sheathing. But if we examine the purpose of the sheathing, which is to protect rather than strengthen, this is inconsequential.

In the case of polyester resins, which tend to be less flexible and shrink to some extent, joints along edges and at ends of cloth should ALWAYS be overlapped by at least two inches or more (at least in single layer applications). Of course, wherever there is an overlap, there will be an additional thickness of material, and in order to not cause a lump or "high spot", the lower layer should be "feathered" or tapered so the transition is gradual. Then the upper layer can be sanded down after the resin cures for a smooth, imperceptible surface. Feather edges just as soon as the resin is hard enough. A disc sander is ideal and fast. But if you wait, the resin just gets harder and there is a greater chance of gouging the adjoining wood.

With butt joints, it can be difficult to keep the cloth tight together at the junction, especially when working with a squeegee which tends to move the cloth around; this can leave gaps at such joints which can be too large. A better way to make the butt joint is to fit the cloth with a slight overlap; it need not be perfectly even. After the resin sets up only partially, cut down the middle of the overlap with a razor knife and remove the excess cloth from both pieces. Lift the cloth on one side to get at the other underneath and replace the fitted portion. You can't wait too long with this method, however. If necessary, a little extra resin can be used as required to re-wet the area.

Edges, corners, and distinct changes in hull form (such as along the chine and keel centerline on vee-bottom hulls, and at the bow) should ordinarily be overlapped at least several inches. This provides a double or triple layer of cloth to reinforce such areas which are ordinarily subjected to considerable abuse in use. Note that edges and corners may tend to absorb and soak up more resin than other areas, especially on sheet plywood boats due to the exposed edge grain. At such areas, it is preferable to pre-coat or apply resin here, wait a moment, and then apply more to compensate.

In many cases, slits or gores will have to be cut in the cloth, especially at corners such as where the bottom, side, and transom join. A corner such as this is probably the most difficult area to cover properly. Another way to provide extra material at edges and corners is to first apply strips of fiberglass cloth tape. Then the sheathing cloth can be lapped onto the previously taped surface.

With fiberglass mat and woven roving, overlapping joints should generally be avoided. The reason is that these materials build up thickness rapidly, and a double layer in an overlapping joint would be

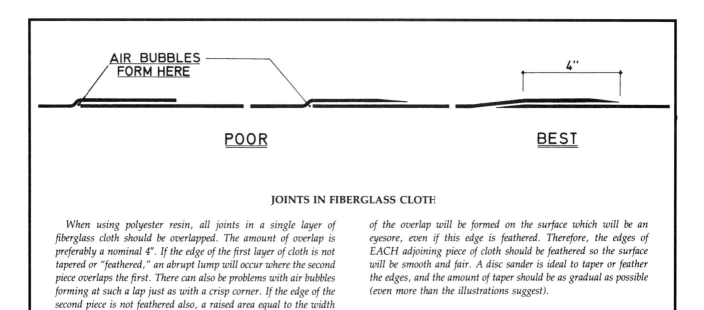

JOINTS IN FIBERGLASS CLOTH

When using polyester resin, all joints in a single layer of fiberglass cloth should be overlapped. The amount of overlap is preferably a nominal 4". If the edge of the first layer of cloth is not tapered or "feathered," an abrupt lump will occur where the second piece overlaps the first. There can also be problems with air bubbles forming at such a lap just as with a crisp corner. If the edge of the second piece is not feathered also, a raised area equal to the width of the overlap will be formed on the surface which will be an eyesore, even if this edge is feathered. Therefore, the edges of EACH adjoining piece of cloth should be feathered so the surface will be smooth and fair. A disc sander is ideal to taper or feather the edges, and the amount of taper should be as gradual as possible (even more than the illustrations suggest).

"lumpy" and difficult to smooth over. When mat and/or woven roving are used, joints are ordinarily butted, and if applied in successive layers, these butt joints are usually staggered so that the butt joints will not fall one above the other and weaken a laminate.

While woven roving joints are butted, the case is a bit different than mat joints. Woven roving does not ordinarily have a selvaged edge as such. Instead, the rovings are loose along the edges, and these loose ends should be lapped and intermingled with each other at junctions for continuity and a smooth transition. Avoid overlapping the PARALLEL strands along the joint as this will form a high spot.

APPLYING TWO LAYERS OF CLOTH

As noted previously, two layers of cloth are sometimes applied, and for best peel strength between the layers, an epoxy resin is preferable. In the case of polyester resin where more protection than that offered by a single layer of cloth is desired, it is better to apply a layer of mat with a single layer of cloth over this, which is described later. However, this combination will tend to weigh more than the double cloth layer, but may not be as costly as a double epoxy cloth application.

While you could apply two layers of cloth, one at a time, this is somewhat like doing the job TWICE. Thus many will prob-

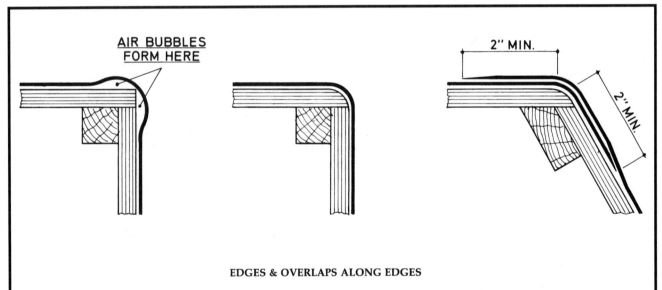

EDGES & OVERLAPS ALONG EDGES

Fiberglass material will not conform to abrupt or crisp edges. The illustration to the left, shows what will occur if the fiberglass material is forced around a "hard" edge. The material will lift off the surface and air bubbles will form. Along such areas, the fiberglass material and resin are useless. The sander will probably go through such an area virtually on contact, or water will get under the area and perhaps leak into the hull or even cause damage to the wood and delamination. This is why all edges should be radiused as shown in the center illustration. Generally, the corners should be radiused as much as possible, but care must be taken so that the joint is not damaged or weakened by hitting the fastenings,

or taking too much ojf of plywood laminations.

The illustration to the right shows a common junction, such as might occur along the chine where the bottom and side planking meet. Usually one piece of material will be used on the bottom, while another piece is used along the side. The two pieces should be lapped as shown. This type of lap is referred to as a "double lap" which will amount to at least 4" of material in two laminations. This amount of lap is a minimum and more is always desirable. Note that the edges of the material in both cases are well "feathered" or tapered to fair into the surface smoothly. The double lap reinforces the junction and makes it virtually leakproof.

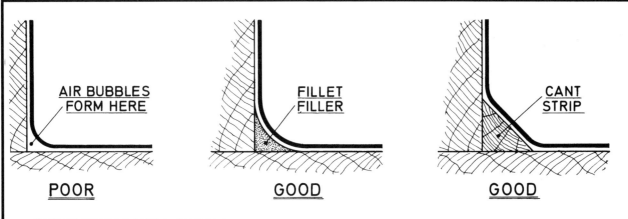

POOR   GOOD   GOOD

HOW TO HANDLE INSIDE CORNERS

Just as fiberglass materials will not bend around a crisp outside corner, so they will not bend into a hard inside corner either. Attempting to do so will cause air bubbles in the corner due to the material lifting and pulling away from the surface. In order to prevent this, the corner should be radiused or fitted with a cant strip in order to minimize the abrupt corner area. The radius can be made from a filler material formed into a concave shape called a fillet.

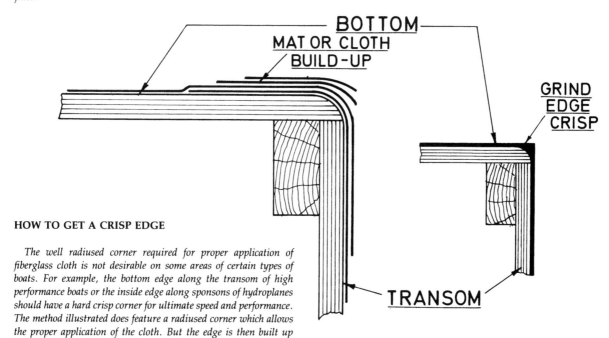

HOW TO GET A CRISP EDGE

The well radiused corner required for proper application of fiberglass cloth is not desirable on some areas of certain types of boats. For example, the bottom edge along the transom of high performance boats or the inside edge along sponsons of hydroplanes should have a hard crisp corner for ultimate speed and performance. The method illustrated does feature a radiused corner which allows the proper application of the cloth. But the edge is then built up with pieces of cloth or mat in order to provide sufficient bulk of fiberglass material and resin so the area can be ground down to form the crisp edge. Enough material should be provided to allow a smooth transition into the adjacent area so the hull lines are straight and true. In other words, the built up area should not form an abrupt "bump" or "hump" at the edge. This could deter from the performance of such a boat. The illustration to the right shows how the completed edge should appear in section view.

ably wonder why they can't apply BOTH layers of cloth in one operation. The answer is that you CAN as long as some different techniques are used.

First, two layers of cloth applied simultaneously should only be attempted if you have some prior experience. There will be too much to contend with for the first-timer, especially on the larger project where this combination might be used. Second, the heavier the cloth, the harder it will be to saturate two layers at once. Cloth heavier than 10-ounce should be avoided for this reason, and the lighter the cloth, the easier it is. Then too, the cloth you will be using, along with the resin, will have some bearing on the job. Make sure that the cloth used wets out quickly and that the resin is capable of doing the same.

Apply two layers at once using the "dry method", and if you insist on using polyester resin, by all means use laminating resin. Do NOT use finish resin, at least on the initial saturating coat. Generally, just about twice as much resin will be required to saturate a given area initially, or put another way, half as much area can be saturated with a given amount of resin using two layers at once, at least for the first saturating coat.

If using polyester resin, always use LESS catalyst than would be used with a single layer as a lot more time will be needed to work the resin through both layers while eliminating wrinkles and air bubbles. Apply the fiberglass cloth layers dry over the bare surface and staple or tack well into position as the cloth will tend to slide about easily.

HOW TO HANDLE CORNERS

Probably one the most difficult areas to cover with fiberglass cloth is a corner where three surfaces join. An example of this is where the side and bottom planking on a hard-chine boat meet the transom. Because three pieces of fiberglass cloth will join over this corner, the cloth must be "gored" or cut to fit around the corner so that excess layers of cloth and resin are not built up. The illustration shows one piece of cloth on the bottom cut with the gore to cover the corner. The lap over and onto the adjoining surface must be at least 2" and preferably more. The pieces of cloth on the sides and the transom are done in a similar manner so that when the application is completed, there will be a triple lamination of cloth over the corner area itself. While the bottom cloth is shown being installed first, the usual method is to install the transom cloth first, and then either the side or the bottom. The angles shown assume a 90° corner on all planes (as if a cube were being covered), and may need to be varied somewhat depending on the adjoining angles.

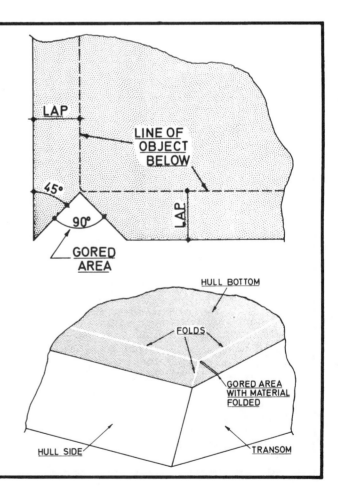

84

TEST PANEL—APPLYING TWO LAYERS OF FIBERGLASS CLOTH AT ONCE

Applying two layers of cloth at one time can be done if some hints are followed (as detailed in the text). Don't use cloth heavier than 10-ounce, always use laminating resin (if using polyester resins) at least for the bonding and saturation, and try to get some experience before sheathing an object as large as a boat.

Apply the cloth using the "dry" method and use somewhat LESS catalyst (if using polyester resin) or use other techniques (if using epoxy resin) to increase cure time. Remember that a given amount of resin will go only about half as far in the initial coat as when using a single layer.

In the photos, the process is shown being done on a test panel. The side surface has been fitted with two layers of cloth and stapled

in place (a). The resin is then applied to saturate and bond the material (b). The brush is being used to keep sufficient resin at the edge area where it tends to drain away.

After setting up, the edge is feathered with a disc sander (c). Then two layers of cloth are fitted and stapled to the bottom surface (d). Resin is poured over the surface and the cloth saturated with a roller (e), although a squeegee may be called for also. A second coat (f) is being applied with the roller to fill the weave of the cloth, and another coat will be applied after to provide a sanding base; resin with surfacing agent or a finish resin containing wax will be used for this last coat when using polyester resin.

Apply a thin coating of resin in several spots around an area of a size that you think can be worked at one time.

Then keep adding resin using a squeegee with a heavy hand. There is a tendency for air bubbles to form under either layer of cloth and these must be worked out together with any wrinkles. Use a roller to level out the resin once down on the surface. The balance of the job is done just the same as any other fiberglass cloth sheathing application.

APPLYING A LAYER OF MAT AND CLOTH

Where extra protection is desired, or where a bare surface has irregularities, it may be desirable to first apply a layer of mat and then cover this with a layer of cloth. Some examples where this might be recommended are on wood strip-cored boats, strip-planked hulls, and double-diagonally planked plywood or solid wood veneer hulls. Polyester resin is recommended for all applications involving mat; not epoxies.

The mat and resin can be applied first to help smooth out rough spots (preferably using a mat roller), and then the cloth can be applied subsequently. However, getting a smooth surface by itself is not easy since mat cannot practically be squeegeed, brush, or rolled with ordinary rollers. Considerable resin will also be required as the result of additional finishing and sanding necessary prior to applying the cloth. The problem is that mat was never intended to form a smooth, high-quality exterior surface. Therefore, it is preferable to apply BOTH mat and cloth layers at once.

To apply both layers at once, fit the materials first and remove. Then lay a section of mat in position and fold it back onto itself. Pour on and/or daub GENEROUS (even ex-

a

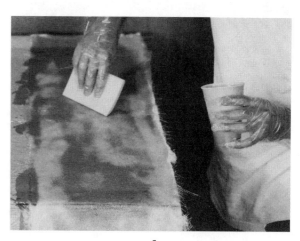
b

TEST PANEL—APPLYING A LAYER OF MAT AND CLOTH AT ONE TIME

Applying a layer of fiberglass mat and cloth at one time can be done as detailed in the text. However, each layer of material must not be too heavy, and it is important that plenty of resin be used initially, coating BOTH sides of the mat in the manner described in the text so resin will be saturating from BOTH sides initially.

This method was NOT used on the test panel and the "dry" areas which show as white spots in (b) are clearly visible, indicating resin-starved areas. All portions of the laminate must be thoroughly saturated to become transparent; this requires a heavy hand with the squeegee and generous amounts of resin.

cess) amounts of resin onto the folded mat and unfold it onto the hull surface. In this way, the resin will be wetting out the mat from the back side first, while more resin can be applied to the mat as required onto the now-exposed surface. This method is preferable to applying the resin just to the surface and then setting the mat into it (as in the "wet method") since the mat will tend to tear apart and be difficult to smooth out.

Do NOT attempt to squeegee or roll out the mat with a roller; use hands only to manipulate the mat roughly into place. Once the mat is largely in place and plenty wet with resin, immediately apply the cloth over the wet mat surface, using a squeegee over the cloth with firm pressure to smooth out both the mat and cloth at the same time. Apply more resin as required to make both layers transparent, however, do not attempt to work too large an area at one time.

The success of this application varies with the weight of the materials used; the lighter each is, the easier the job. About a 1-ounce mat and a 10-ounce cloth should be considered maximum, especially for the beginner. It is also preferable to NOT do this type of job alone; the more help the better since plenty of resin must be mixed AND made readily available in a hurry AND applied quickly. It is important that resin be applied to BOTH sides of the mat initially, using the folding method described. The success of the job is based on the premise of the wet mat helping saturate the overlying cloth. The balance of the job is otherwise the same as a fiberglass cloth sheathing application.

APPLYING A LAYER OF MAT AND WOVEN ROVING

Very seldom are mat and woven roving applied together as a sheathing since such a heavy, coarse laminate is seldom necessary or desirable. Besides, getting a good

finished surface is tedious. While separate materials can be used, combination materials which include layers of both mat and woven roving are available. In either case, these can be applied simultaneously as long as the labor is available, or mat and woven roving layers can be applied separately.

Photo shows fiberglass mat with woven roving being laid over it as might be the case in a heavy sheathing build-up. Note that woven roving does not have a selvaged edge as is the case with fiberglass cloth.

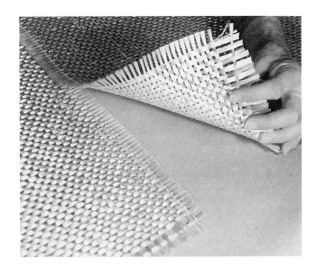

The loose ends of fiberglass woven roving should be lapped and intermingled with each other at junctions for strength continuity.

In such a sheathing, polyester laminating resin is used, with the mat against the surface initially. Epoxy resins are not advised. Basically, the mat portion is applied in the same manner described for application of a layer of mat and cloth. In other words, the mat is folded onto itself so that resin will be wetting out the material from front and back. The woven roving is applied in a similar fashion over the mat using plenty of resin that is preferably under-catalyzed to increase working time. Considerable resin

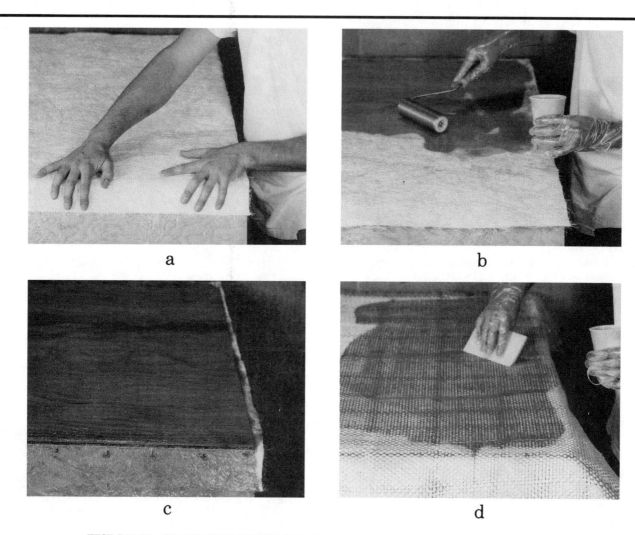

a

b

c

d

TEST PANEL—HEAVY-DUTY FIBERGLASS SHEATHING WITH MAT AND WOVEN ROVING

Where extra protection is more important than added weight or surface quality, a surface can be covered with a layer of mat and woven roving, with the mat applied against the surface initially. Polyester laminating resin is used throughout except for the final sanding coat. The beginner should not attempt to apply these layers together at one time. The mat is used first since it makes a better bond. Note the mat roller being used in (b). Once totally saturated and while still wet (c), the woven roving can be applied over it.

With both layers, the material should be folded back onto itself

with resin applied to both the front and back sides so that resin will be saturating from both sides. Alternately with the mat, the substrate surface could be coated with resin first as in the "wet" method for a similar effect. Plenty of resin will be required so somewhat less catalyst should be used to allow more working time. Note the rough surface in (d); this will require considerably more resin to permit sanding, along with finishing techniques described in the text, or alternately, another thin layer of mat could be used, but this would make a heavy laminate that would be difficult to finish in a "yachtlike" manner.

build-up, or the use of resins mixed with filler materials, is required to conceal the weave of the woven roving. Alternately, you could add another layer of mat and do fairing on this, but this would add more weight, work, and expense. Otherwise finishing techniques are similar to other combinations of materials.

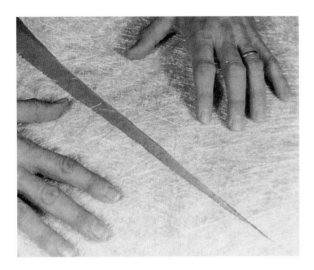

a

b

Joints in fiberglass mat can be butted as shown in (a). However, there is no harm in having joints made as in (b). In fact, tearing the mat to form a ragged edge as in (b) is actually stronger than in (a) once the two pieces have been melded together and wetted out with resin. The joint in either approach is easy to conceal.

CHOPPER GUN SHEATHING APPLICATIONS

The following technique is not applicable to beginners and is even questionable for the experienced. Basically, the technique involves the use of what is called a "chopper gun". This is a piece of equipment commonly used by fiberglass fabricators which feeds fiberglass rovings through a nozzle where they are chopped into short strands and mixed with catalyzed polyester resin at the same time. This "mix" is shot out onto a surface (usually against a female mold for some part) with the depth of the laminate controlled by the operator of the gun.

Since the female mold surface determines the quality of the final surface of the part in this process, the exposed side being shot by the gun is necessarily quite rough, but not necessarily uneven. To complete the laminate so deposited, a worker must use a mat roller. Such a process has been attempted for exterior sheathing work and can be done if the skill and equipment are available. However, finish work will be tedious and such a sheathing will tend to add weight and thickness quickly. Such a coating should be durable, and perhaps best suited to a workboat application where a flawless surface is unimportant.

SHEATHING APPLICATION VARIATIONS USING EPOXY ENCAPSULATION SYSTEMS

One of the most important advancements in wood boat construction, especially from the standpoint of the amateur boatbuilder, has been the development of epoxy encapsulating resins. These boatbuilding resins form a "system" of boat construction used not only to glue and hold all members together, but also to coat and seal, or "encapsulate", each and every part of the boat's structure. The plastic epoxy literally seals out moisture, and therefore rot, worms, and insects. This, in turn, strengthens a hull, reduces maintenance, increases boat life, minimizes weight, and eliminates leaks. The boat literally becomes a wood-epoxy "composite" much stronger and more durable than ordinary wood and one that's covered inside and out by a highly impermeable coating.

However, as durable as the epoxy coating may be, exterior hull surfaces still need the protection offered by a fiberglass or comparable material sheathing. The sheathing not only gives all the benefits afforded to any other boat so covered, but it protects the epoxy encapsulating coating against penetration by foreign objects and collisions. The fiberglass provides a hardness that the epoxy alone cannot, even though it may be tough compared to other coatings such as paint. In addition, the cloth acts as a screed on the outside to assure a minimum thickness coating. If it were not there, you could sand away too much of the epoxy coating and lose the benefits of encapsulation.

The fiberglass sheathing in this building method also often adds some degree of strength and stiffening, particularly at junctions where the fibers of the sheathing material run across the joint. In many designs using this method of construction, soft woods such as Western red cedar may be used for the planking. The fiberglass sheathing gives this fairly soft wood a more durable surface while increasing impact strength.

The encapsulating resin used for the system is usually also used for the sheathing application without modification. There is really only one difference or variation in applying sheathing applications from that described in the "dry method".

A seal coat of epoxy is applied to the bare wood surface BEFORE applying the cloth. A thin foam roller is used in long, multi-directional strokes with good pressure to keep this first coat as thin as possible to prevent runs and sags or high and low spots. After about 10 to 15 minutes, the surface is checked for any dry spots where the wood has absorbed the resin, especially over edge and end-grain areas, and more applied accordingly.

The resin for this seal coat is to make sure that all areas of the hull's structure get covered with the encapsulating resin and sealed, especially areas which will tend to soak up resin. Air escaping from the wood may cause small bubbles to appear. This is a proper occurrence and indicates proper sealing; too thick a coat will inhibit this reaction. The resin coat should be worked as long as possible to assure that all areas are evenly coated. Work from a dryer area to a wetter area; there is no need to stop. However, don't recoat an area if it has begun to set up.

Allow the coat to cure at least tack-free (or even overnight) before doing subsequent work on the surface. The surface may appear fuzzy upon cure, which is usually of no consequence. However, if runs and sags or EXTREME roughness occurs in an area of a type that would interfere with the easy and smooth application of the cloth, these areas should be sanded. However, heavy power sanding on this coat should be avoided to prevent removing the seal coat or damaging the wood surface.

A light hand sanding plus perhaps a solvent wipe should be all that's necessary prior to the cloth application. In lieu of sanding, some use a cabinet scraper and these also work well. However, an absolutely smooth surface is not necessary. Although sanding is not technically necessary for bonding purposes to the next coat, this will assure the removal of any possible surface contamination or amine blush resulting from a complete cure. The surface should be clean, dry, and free of dust. Some prefer to wait and do any filling of holes until AFTER this first seal coat is applied. This is acceptable with epoxy resin if desired, or they can be taken care of in the usual manner. Cloth application can otherwise be done in the normal manner after the seal coat has cured and been prepared as noted.

USING WOOD PRESERVATIVES

Wood preservatives are often used in wood boatbuilding and many want to know if these are compatible with resin. This is a complex subject. First, if the boat in question has been built with an epoxy encapsulation system, the use of preservative is NOT usually advocated. Since the wood is theoretically sealed in epoxy, there is simply no need for preservatives. In these cases, should a wood surface become damaged and exposed to possible rot, a repair coating of more epoxy will eliminate this potential.

In other cases, a prerequisite for a successful sheathing application is that the resin be applied over a BARE wood surface; that is, one which has NOT been coated with ANYTHING including wood preservatives. Many preservatives are in petroleum-based solvents, and while these may dry out after time, bonding to such a surface would always be questionable, especially if using polyester resin. Besides, once a surface is sheathed, there is little chance of rot, at least from the side that is covered. Thus applying wood preservatives to surfaces that are to be sheathed is largely a waste and questionable practice.

However, there may be other circumstances. For example, inner hull surfaces which may NOT be covered with resin can be coated with preservatives, and when flooding these on, there may be a chance that the preservative will pass through joints and get on surfaces that are to be sheathed. If this occurs to a large extent (it shouldn't if your joints are well glued, tight, and sound), bonding problems could occur, especially with polyester resins.

Thus it may be advisable to make a test panel, applying the preservative and letting it dry thoroughly, then applying a sheath-ing sample to see if an adequate bond develops. If bonding problems do occur with polyester resin, perhaps the sample did not dry long enough. If this is not the case, then test with epoxy resins, which should bond better. If this doesn't work, avoid using the particular preservative.

FINISHING

When applying sheathing materials, only as much resin as necessary to saturate, bond, conceal the weave, and provide a sanding base should be used. More resin than this can lead to cracking or delamination due to resin richness; a thick build-up will not be properly reinforced by the sheathing material and does not mean more strength.

Once the sheathing material weave has been concealed, finish coats of resin can be applied. If using polyester resin, these should be made with finish resin, although a PVA mold release could also be used with a laminating resin, but this is not common.

The final resin coat should be no thicker than is required to develop a smooth, even surface. If you have been careful throughout the application, one such coat will suffice. However, don't be afraid to use more coats if necessary since final coats will be sanded and enough resin should be applied to prevent cutting through to the sheathing material.

Pigment may be added to the final coat, but the primary reason for doing this will be to better show up any uneven spots and to assure a more even final coat. When using finish resin for the final coat, especially with pigment, a brush can be used optionally after roller application to smooth out the stipple effect of the roller. However, don't expect to eliminate sanding by this process.

The amount of sanding that will be required depends on the quality of the final surface which is acceptable by the worker.

If the quality of the surface prior to applying the finish coat has excessive sanding marks, gouges, or other imperfections, these will NOT be hidden by the final coats. These defects must be eliminated or otherwise "covered up" if a top quality finish is desired.

For correcting less-than-perfect surfaces, there are three approaches. The first method is to build up finish coats and sand each until defects are eliminated. Before sanding, always make sure there is sufficient resin. A value judgement will have to be made of the surface quality before sanding to determine the grade or coarseness of sandpaper to start with. Don't use too coarse a paper and put in deeper marks than already exist. However, with this approach you will have to graduate progressively to finer papers as sanding proceeds, eventually ending up with finish instead of disc or belt sanders.

On surfaces that are initially not as smooth as they could be, or where the worker wants to save "elbow grease", a couple of other approaches can be tried, both of which apply to hulls that will eventually be painted. One approach involves sanding the surfaces down to a fairly even, smooth surface, but not necessarily one free of sanding or grinding marks. Instead of attempting to build up the surface with resin and sanding these coats smooth, a high-build primer undercoat is sprayed, brushed, or rolled on the surface to fill these defects. The primer surface is then sanded smooth and finally painted. This type of primer is usually made for easy sanding and can be sprayed or applied in a continuous manner so that the buildup can be thick to conceal defects. Then sanding is performed on the surface as required, which is much easier than sanding resin. Painting is done after.

The third approach is best used on really unfair surfaces where it is impractical to build up resin or primer undercoats sufficiently. This involves the use of a resin fill

coat which is made by mixing microspheres with the finish coats of resin much as was discussed in Chapter 8, concerning fillers you can make yourself.

In this method, the microspheres are added until a resin filler is developed to a

For application of resin filler coats, a wide trowel or screed can be used to apply the material as is being done here.

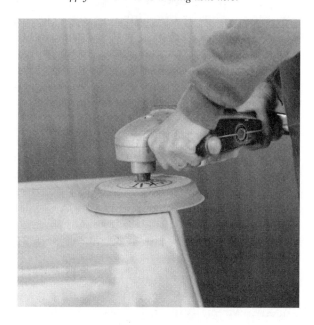

Resin filler coats must be sanded fair for a smooth, even surface prior to painting. A foam-backed sanding disc such as shown will minimize gouging the surface.

batter consistency. This is applied to the surface with a notched trowel such as is used to apply linoleum adhesive, or some use an old saw blade. Since most of the fill coat will be sanded off, the alternating high and low streaks give a visual indication of the coating thickness remaining as it is sanded, as well as some idea of where high and low areas exist. The streaks also make sanding easier since there is not as much material to sand as would be the case with a solid coat. This type of filler coat is the same approach used for fairing fiberglass hulls built with "one-off" male mold methods. The microspheres make sanding easy and quick, but still such coatings should be no thicker than necessary. Surfaces can be primed and/or painted after.

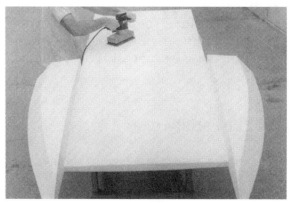

One way to build up a sheathed surface in lieu of tedious sanding is to use a high-build undercoat/primer. Most can be sprayed while some can actually be applied with a putty knife as is being done here. Such primers can be readily sanded with finish sanders after they dry. The principle of this method is to do sanding on the primer rather than on the harder resin.

CLEAR TRANSPARENT COATINGS

A clear, transparent surface is commonly desired to show a natural wood surface below. To eliminate as much sanding as possible, considerable care should be taken in the sheathing application. Some "tips" that will be of help are given in the following.

First, if you want a clear finish, thinner cloth such as 4- or 6-ounce is preferable. Thicker cloths will tend to show the weave and are harder to wet out without leaving white spots. If you have precoated a wood surface to remain clear PRIOR to applying any cloth, take care NOT to sand through the resin coating; the sanded wood area will be appreciably lighter in color even if re-coated, and could be visible in the end.

When applying the cloth, keep handling to a minimum to prevent fractured strands. Be careful using the squeegee and keep this to a minimum to prevent damaging the cloth. Rounding off the corners of the squeegee also helps in this regard. Remove any loose strands after the cloth has been draped in position; some use a vacuum cleaner for this operation. If globs of milky-colored loose or fractured strands occur, pluck them off the wet surface. Milkiness in the resin can be caused by air becoming trapped in the resin as it is moved around in the saturation process. Some avoid the use of rollers for this reason and use a squeegee throughout, but this requires a special knack to minimize squeegee marks.

On many wood surfaces, the resin itself will give a good deep grain color. However, in some cases of grain variation or undesired color, some may want to stain the wood surface first. If this is desired, an oil-based stain or water-based vinyl stain which will peel off must NOT be used. The only stain which is acceptable is an alcohol-based stain that may not be easy to find. Always make a discardable test sample first before staining an area to determine if the results are what you are looking for.

Procedures for obtaining a clear transparent finish are otherwise the same as for any sheathing application. The only difference is that because a clear surface is desired, more work will be required in sanding, using fine papers and eventually working up to "wet-or-dry" papers and perhaps even buffing with automotive cutting compounds and polishes or rottenstone abrasive for the ultimate finish.

Bare resin surfaces are not very durable over time and will eventually deteriorate in the sun due to ultraviolet degradation. Thus a protective finish, such as an ultraviolet inhibited varnish or urethane coating is necessary, applied per the manufacturer's recommendations. Such coatings can usually be brushed or sprayed on, and will require periodic recoating as often as yearly if exposure is constant and severe.

PAINTING

When the desired degree of surface smoothness has been reached, the surface can be painted if a clear finish is not desired as already described. Actually, the terminology "paint" should be referred to as a "coating" because many of the modern marine coatings involve rather complex formulations that are actually "systems" of products used in a certain sequence, and do not much resemble ordinary paints of the past.

Because of the wide variety of coating systems available, be sure that the system is compatible with the sheathing application. Most modern marine products available today will fall into this category, but don't attempt to use ordinary water-base products that you would use in your house. And regardless of the product used, ALWAYS follow the manufacturer's instructions TO THE LETTER. Do NOT vary from the procedures or intermix products except on the advice of experts. Regardless of the paint system used, WAIT AT LEAST 48 HOURS BEFORE PAINTING IF POLYESTER RESIN HAS BEEN USED, AND AT LEAST 7 DAYS IF EPOXY RESIN HAS BEEN USED; this will assure that the resin has cured adequately.

If the system calls for a primer, it may be possible to tint this to the final color; this will make dings or scratches less obvious. Or if a primer is not specified or required, the resin can be pigmented as noted previously for the same effect.

In many cases, it is not necessary to paint the bottom of hulls, especially those which will not remain in salt or brackish waters, or for boats which will be trailered. Because the bottom surface is not exposed to the sun and will be in the water when the boat is subject to exposure, adding paint in these cases is merely done for cosmetic reasons except where an anti-fouling bottom paint is necessary.

From a practical standpoint, the clear resin surface on the bottom also makes inspection of the fiberglassed surface easy as any faults or tendency to delaminate can be quickly spotted. In areas where water may get behind the fiberglass cloth and wood hull material, a dark smudge or black area will show the path of the water on sight. If the hull were painted, it would be difficult if not impossible to spot such a defect. Also, a clear coating makes it easy to see any fastenings, fractures, or other structural defects in the underlying structure which would otherwise be concealed by a painted surface.

NON-SKID SURFACES

Non-skid surfaces are easy to achieve for areas such as decks and cabin tops. These can be incorporated in the final resin coat or in the paint finish. Essentially, the process involves broadcasting a suitable non-skid material into the final coat. There are special non-skid materials available (often some sort of ground walnut shell) or sand of a type used in children's sandboxes. This latter material may be too coarse, and a finer abrasive sand material may be substituted of a type available from concrete specialty trade suppliers. You can make tests to check your preferences.

Applying resin with a thin foam roller provides an excellent base for receiving the non-skid material since it lays down a coating that will not be so thick as to bury the non-skid material. You can pigment the resin beforehand if desired. Mask off any areas where you don't want the non-skid pattern. Broadcast the non-skid material with a salt shaker or an insecticide spray duster. Don't attempt to do this by hand since it's too difficult to control.

MISCELLANEOUS APPLICATION TIPS

On surfaces where resin and sheathing materials are being applied, there may be adjacent surfaces on which you don't want any resin. For example, it's common on vee bottom boats to do the bottom and then the sides or vice versa. There will usually be an overlap along the chine of several inches. Yet when resin is applied on the bottom (assuming the boat is upside down), you want to keep resin from running onto the sides whether this area has been covered yet or not.

To do this, cover the sides beyond the overlap area with newspaper or kraft paper, and tape continuously in place with masking tape. If the surface is not protected this way, the resin will drain down onto the sides and you'll probably be too busy doing other things before it will set up and cure in a mess. When the surface is protected properly, a utility knife can be used to cut along BOTH the tape and the overhanging fiberglass cloth edge for a clean, neat edge that can be feathered later for a proper overlap.

Although fiberglass material can be applied to an area and cut to shape initially,

There is a point in the cure cycle of resin that's ideal for trimming off overhanging material. If the resin has not set up enough, the cloth will pull away. If the resin sets up too much, it will not be possible to cut it. Here a sharp utility knife is being used at just the right time to trim off excess material.

there is no reason why this cannot be done AFTER the resin has been applied in most cases, unless you must cut the material in advance for optimum material utilization. The best tool to use is a utility knife or razor blade knife with a sharp blade (fiberglass will dull blades quickly so have a good supply ready).

However, there is a "right" time to cut any overhanging "wet" edges, and this is neither too late nor too soon. If you try to cut the material too soon, not only will it not cut, but the material will drag along the surface thereby displacing it, and it will have to be rolled or squeegeed down again. If you wait too long to trim, the resin will simply be too hard and the knife just won't cut.

The "right" time to trim the material is just before the resin sets up hard, yet is "stiff" enough to keep the material in position. This "right" time is about an hour after application under normal conditions if using polyester resin. For epoxy resin, the

This photo shows the assembly of the centerboard trunk halves in a small sailboat. Fiberglass sheathing is applied to the inside trunk surfaces for protection. Thus each half must be covered with fiberglass cloth and resin PRIOR to final assembly. Each half is covered in the usual manner; then they are joined and fastened while the resin is still wet. No glue is necessary since the wet resin will bond the two halves together and the fastenings will provide the necessary clamping pressure. This method is especially effective with epoxy resin. For polyester resin, a better bond and seal at the joint will result if the mating surfaces are fitted with a thin layer of saturated mat in addition to the cloth.

principle is the same but times may vary more; make a check of your conditions. When trimming partially cured material, you can keep the blade clean and sharper longer by rinsing in solvent.

Of course, there are many places where a disc sander can be used to trim edges once the resin does cure. And it is possible to cut cloth with scissors. In this case, the cloth can be cut while it is still wet. You must lift it off the surface to do this, but as long as the resin is still wet enough, it's easy to push it back in place, although you can't wait too long with this method. Make sure any resin is cleaned from the scissors with solvent before it sets up.

If any fiberglass material is being held in place with tacks or staples, these must be removed before the resin sets up hard also. If staples are driven just a bit "cockeyed", they will be easier to remove. Just as noted above, you can remove tacks and staples too soon, especially on vertical surfaces. The sheathing material may then slide down the surface or otherwise move.

When doing a large project, have at least TWO sets of application tools so that one set can be used while the other set is being cleaned and readied for the next use. Once a batch of resin starts to gel, the remaining resin batch is not only discarded, but the reusable tools should be cleaned before using with a fresh batch of resin.

Rollers and brushes can be cleaned, but it is seldom worth it; the solvent or cleaner probably costs as much or more than these tools, and it takes valuable time. Many squeegees can be left in solvent, but other types can dry out and get hard. If squeegees are to be reused, they should be cleaned in solvent, washed in detergent water, and then dried, or follow instructions provided.

Sooner or later the solvent used for cleaning will begin to accumulate too much resin, and because the resin has been catalyzed, it may even tend to set up and cure. It is even possible for the curing resin in the solvent to get hot enough to be dangerous. This tendency seems to be more prevalent when using acetone due to its high rate of evaporation, and this is another recommendation for less volatile thinners such as lacquer thinner, or better yet, resin cleaners. For safety, volatile solvent should be stored in closable metal containers.

PROBLEMS-SOLUTIONS & PREVENTION

The following is a representative sampling of the more common problems which can arise. It is by no means a comprehensive listing of all problems that can occur, as these can be unique to a given situation and defy analysis or cause. Also, some obvious conditions have not been listed. For example, the fact that old resin, hardener, or catalyst can be responsible for just about any of the resin problems listed; this is why fresh products are important. In solving the following problems, it should be noted that the solutions and preventions almost always consider proper application methods and care for satisfactory results. Keep in mind that virtually any application mistake can be corrected, albeit at some degree of work and expense.

FINISH PROBLEMS

CONDITION	POSSIBLE CAUSES	SOLUTIONS/PREVENTION
A. Surface "blushing"	1. Surface immersed in water too soon 2. Uncured surface exposed to wet night air, fog, dew, etc.	1. Let surface cure as prescribed 2. Avoid damp conditions during cure
B. Material delamination	1. Air bubbles in material 2. Material improperly applied 3. Surface improperly prepared 4. Resin not cured 5. Defective fabric 6. Improper fabric finish 7. Wax not removed from finish resin between coats	1. For satisfactory job, ALL application procedures must be carefully done and quality material used
C. Paint will not adhere to surface	1. Wax not removed from final resin coat 2. Amine blush on surface with epoxy 3. Paint system not properly applied or selected 4. Resin not fully cured or finish resin not used in final coat (if using polyester resin)	1. Sand surface adequately before applying paint 2. Wipe down surface with damp rag 3. Use compatible paint system 4. Allow resin to cure at least 48 hours; use finish resin (polyester resin)
D. Resin surface comes off	1. Resin rich area not adequately reinforced 2. Resin applied over contaminated or wet surface, or over polyester finish resin not sanded	1. Apply resin evenly 2. Be sure surface is clean, dry, and free of wax
E. Cratering, pin holes, or "fisheyes" develop	1. Surface contaminated 2. Weather too hot and/or humid 3. Products not agitated	1. Be sure surface is clean 2. Work in better conditions 3. Agitate containers before mixing

POLYESTER RESINS:

CONDITION	POSSIBLE CAUSES	SOLUTIONS/PREVENTION
A. Resin not curing	1. Catalyst not added 2. Insufficient catalyst added 3. Conditions too cold	1. Add catalyst 2. Check amount of catalyst used and try adding more 3. Increase working temperatures; use a "cold weather" resin
B. Spotty curing	1. Improper mixing of catalyst	1. Stir catalyst for at least 2 minutes 2. Improperly shaped mixing container
C. Surface too tacky	1. Resin thinned, or applied under damp or cold conditions	1. Do NOT thin resin, or apply under damp conditions, or cure under 60°F without using "cold weather" resin
D. Too rapid curing	1. Too much catalyst 2. Ambient temperatures too high	1. Reduce amount of catalyst used 2. Apply on cooler day
E. Slow curing	1. Not enough catalyst 2. Ambient temperatures too low	1. Use more catalyst 2. Apply on warmer day
F. Partially tacky surface	1. Excessive brushing at time of gelation	1. Do NOT over-brush surface or brush after gelation begins
G. Resin hard or coagulating in can	1. Resin too old 2. Contaminated catalyst	1. Discard resin and use fresh stock 2. Discard resin batch and use fresh catalyst

EPOXY RESINS:

CONDITION	POSSIBLE CAUSES	SOLUTIONS/PREVENTION
A. Resin not curing	1. Used only Part "A" or Part "B" 2. Used improper ratios	1. Mix parts in proper ratio 2. Remove and discard material
B. Spotty curing	1. Insufficient mixing	1. Stir for at least 2 minutes 2. Improperly shaped mixing container
C. Slight tacky surface	1. Conditions too damp or humid	1. Do not apply in damp or humid conditions
D. Too rapid curing	1. Ambient temperatures too high	1. Apply on a cooler day
E. Slow curing	1. Ambient temperatures too low 2. Improper mixing	1. Apply on a warmer day 2. Mix properly
F. Final surface flexible	1. Mixing proportions not correct	1. Mix per instructions

FIBERGLASS MATERIAL:

CONDITIONS	POSSIBLE CAUSES	SOLUTIONS/PREVENTION
A. Bubbles forming on wet surface	1. Insufficient wet-out 2. Material moving on surface	1. Work bubbles out with application tools 2. Tack or staple materials adequately to prevent movement or change application tool or technique
B. Bubbles on cured surface	1. Insufficient wet-out 2. Material movement 3. Vigorous or excessive stirring of resin	1. Sand or grind out bubble and replace with material patch and fresh resin – applies to all causes
C. Excessively dry or wet areas	1. Insufficient resin distribution	1. Add resin to dry areas and squeegee out wet areas before resin sets up
D. Partial bonding	1. Contaminated surface 2. Wax not removed from coated surface 3. Amine blush not removed on cured epoxy surface	1. Prepare surface properly 2. Sand and wash surface with solvent to remove wax when using polyester finish resin 3. Wipe down surface with damp rag

PART 2

INTRODUCTION

Fiberglass is not the only sheathing material that can be used in boat work, and some feel that it is not even the best choice, at least for all applications. Other sheathing materials are available that can be used with resin in much the same manner as fiberglass. There is also at least one sheathing process that does not use either polyester or epoxy resin. In addition, there is a special process that can be used for restoring old wood boats.

Several of these alternative materials will be discussed in the following, along with their merits and disadvantages, so that the reader can better make a choice based on his needs and requirements. These materials include polypropylene fabrics (or "Vectra" as it is more commonly known), modacrylic fiber fabric (better known as "Dynel"), a process using various fabric sheathings applied with a polyvinyl glue-like product called "Arabol", and a boat restoration process using a fiberglass material called "C-FLEX".

CHAPTER 10   Polypropylene Fabric

To the novice, polypropylene fabric looks just like fiberglass cloth, and in most sheathing applications, it can be used in the same way, such as for hulls, decks, and cabins. It has some purported advantages over fiberglass cloth as well as Dynel fabric that will be discussed later.

"Vectra" is the popular name given to polypropylene fabrics because the Vectra Company first made the polypropylene olefin fiber that later was woven into fabrics by other firms. One such fabric was "Versatex", and the product is also known by this name. To keep things simple, the term Vectra will be used in the following.

Vectra is much lighter in weight than fiberglass for comparable coverings, and even lighter than Dynel. Vectra fabric weighing approximately 4-ounces per square yard can be substituted for fiberglass cloth weighing 10-ounces per square yard and will require similar amounts of resin as this weight of fiberglass cloth to yield coverings of similar thicknesses. However, because of the lighter fabric, this means lighter sheathing applications and lighter boats, at least in theory. Abrasion and impact resistance, flexibility, and adhesion are supposedly better than with fiberglass.

However, some who have experience with many sheathing materials dispute the claims about adhesion or "peel strength" in particular. Their experience with plastic cloths such as polypropylene show that it is extremely difficult to bond to; they claim that only a mechanical "keying"—type of bond results, leading to low peel strength values. However, the literature on Vectra claims peel strength values considerably higher than fiberglass when used on various wood substrates. Such controversy makes it difficult for the consumer to resolve. If it is any consolation, peel strength is probably adequate for most uses, especially if epoxy resins are used.

The elasticity of Vectra allows the fabric to stretch more than fiberglass without cracking (although the resin used and the type of hull structure will have some bearing on this quality as will be discussed). Unlike fiberglass when being sanded, Vectra is non-irritating and non-allergenic, an important point to some sensitive workers (although again, the resin used may negate these qualities for some workers to a certain extent).

Vectra fabrics are not nearly as common as fiberglass and the cost is generally much higher. Part of this problem may be due to the fact that the material has no place in molded fiberglass boat construction; its primary use is as a sheathing material. This limits demand and distribution considerably. However, unlike Dynel, the fabric can be used as a composite "one-off" boatbuilding material as demonstrated by the boat shown in the photos, although fiberglass cloth can serve the same purpose, but at some increase in weight.

The use of Vectra, however, is not trouble-free, and much controversy and strong opinion exists about its use. One of the most commonly mentioned problems is also one of its attributes. The light weight of the fabric (which keeps boat weight down while adding some inherent buoyancy) causes it to "float" if too much resin is applied, leading to application problems.

While it would seem easy enough to limit the resin to an amount that would be sufficient to bond the fabric and yet not allow it to raise above the surface, this can be a problem when working on relatively large areas, AND within the time limits imposed by resin on its way to setting up, AND while still attempting to wet out the fabric properly so that no bubbles or wrinkles will form.

A survey of professional users made in preparation of this text showed that this was the main complaint of those dependent on making a profit in working with sheathing systems. They could not afford the problems associated with the use of Vectra, and hence most avoided the material in favor of simpler, cheaper fiberglass.

Unlike fiberglass cloth which is supple and will not wrinkle, Vectra fabric will hold a crease, thereby making it difficult to keep the fabric onto the surface in the vicinity of the wrinkle until the resin sets up. For this reason, the fabric should be purchased in roll form and not folded.

If a wrinkle or crease does exist, lay cellophane or other parting film against the surface and hold it down by hand or with weights until the resin sets. However, this practice can be a nuisance or even impractical on a large surface with numerous wrinkles.

Finishing Vectra fabric also present problems, especially in the normal method of application where resin is used to wet out and build up thickness to conceal the fabric weave. When feathering a lap joint, the material tends to "fuzz" when sanded, unlike fiberglass cloth which will blend into a smooth taper. The same holds true if you inadvertently sand through the resin and into the fabric.

With fiberglass, the area need only be recoated with more resin and a patch of cloth fitted in place. The Vectra material does not work this way, and indeed the recommended procedure is NOT to lap any joints, but rather butt them. On a single layer this will leave a break in the reinforcing, and if such is not desired, a second layer of material is required, with butt joints staggered between layers.

However, as with fiberglass cloth, peel strength is poor if using more than two layers of fabric unless epoxy resin is used. While either polyester or epoxy resins may be used with Vectra, in order to realize the material's ability to stretch without cracking, epoxy resins are again preferable over more rigid polyesters. Of course, this adds further to the cost of the total sheathing application.

To minimize the tendency for the material to "float", it can be applied "dry" to the surface, cut to rough size, stapled in position, and then saturated with a minimum amount of resin applied over. Conditions that will lead to a fairly rapid resin cure time (e.g. warmer temperatures or extra catalyst if polyester resin is used) are often recommended in order to keep the material down on the surface with less effort.

Another approach is sometimes used with Vectra to prevent both the "floating" problem and the "fuzzing" problem with sanding. Instead of applying with the "dry" method, a technique more like the "wet" method is employed. A coating of epoxy resin is applied to the surface, recoating dry spots where required, until the surface is uniformly glossy. The pre-cut fabric, which has been rolled onto a tube or dowel, is unrolled into the wet resin and smoothed out much the same as in a fiberglass cloth application.

The resin saturates the fabric, and if areas remain opaque, more resin is applied. However, excessive resin (indicated by a glossy surface) should be avoided as this will cause the cloth to float, slide around, and develop wrinkles. Do not attempt to fill in the weave of the cloth with the resin, however, as one would do with fiberglass cloth. The resin is used in this technique only to wet out the cloth and bond it to the surface.

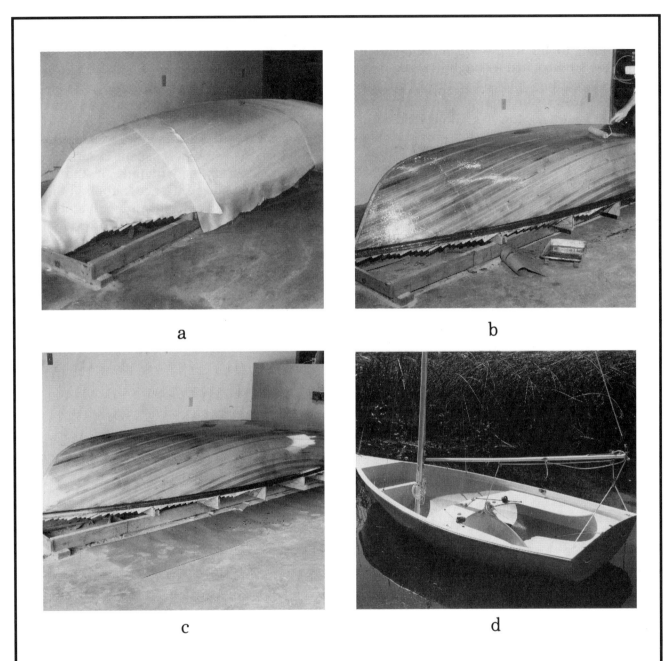

a

b

c

d

USING POLYPROPYLENE FABRIC OVER A WOOD STRIP SANDWICH CORE

This series of photos show the building of a "one-off" boat (the "GLEN-L 11") using a core of wood strip planking edge nailed (but not necessarily glued) together over temporary transverse male mold frames which will be removed later. Ordinary light-weight, inexpensive wood, such as shelving pine, can be used for the core. It is not necessary that the strips be full length. The outer sheer member is sprung around the hull and bonded to the wood strips.

Two layers of polypropylene cloth are then applied over the outside. Joints in the cloth are butted and staggered between layers. When the outer laminate is completed, the hull can be righted and the temporary members removed. The interior is then also covered with two layers of polypropylene cloth. The resulting boat is free of frames, forming a "stress skin" or "monocoque" sandwich core structure that is quite strong yet not heavy. While poly-propylene fabric was used in this case, fiberglass cloth could also be substituted.

Instead, an epoxy surfacing compound (a paste-like filler) is applied over the cured sheathing to fill in the weave and build up the surface just enough for sanding without cutting into the cloth. Paint or other coatings can be applied after in the typical manner. However, note that with this method, a clear finish is not possible since the filler is opaque.

A criticism of this technique is that to overcome the difficulty in sanding, a thicker resin build-up is required than is the case with using resin alone, as is done with fiberglass cloth. This means that much of the purported weight advantage of Vectra is negated.

Another criticism of Vectra is that while the material is strong, high strength is not developed until the material is stretched. Thus, in the case of more rigid forms of wood construction, such as cold-molded or plywood hulls, the wood structure to which the material is usually bonded would break before the strength of the Vectra could be realized. Hence, although the material is suitable for sheathing, it adds nothing in the way of practical reinforcement or stiffness.

CHAPTER 11

Modacrylic Fiber Fabric

The term "modacrylic" is popularly known as "Dynel", a trade name developed by Union Carbide Corporation for a fiber that can be woven into cloth and used very much in the same manner as fiberglass cloth. However, Dynel (as we'll refer to it here for simplicity) comes in "staple fiber" form as compared to monofilaments such as fiberglass and polypropylene. Staple fiber is made from relatively short lengths that are spun and twisted into yarn having a fuzzy quality, whereas monofilaments are made in continuous lengths of fiber bundles which are parallel to each other. The importance of this characteristic will be explained later.

Dynel arrived on the scene somewhat before polypropylene, but was never touted as a construction material to replace fiberglass as such. Instead, it was promoted as an "overlay" or sheathing material that offered qualities superior to fiberglass in many respects. Although it gained some early acceptance because of its drapeability, softness, abrasion resistance, and superior toughness, it never really gave fiberglass any major competition for several reasons, even though it does still have a place in the world of sheathings.

One can compare fiberglass to Dynel to spot its unique characteristics. Dynel has a breaking tensile strength of 40,000 to 50,000 pounds per square inch with an elongation of about 35%. Fiberglass, on the other hand, has a breaking tensile strength of 300,000 pounds per square inch at an elongation of only 3 to 4%. Where the fiberglass fabric gives high ultimate strength, the Dynel fabric will stretch and elongate con-

siderably more before failing. Hence, the ability of Dynel to withstand scrapes and abrasions without failure; this is how it gets its reputation as being "tough". However, its impact resistance is not as good as fiberglass, and considerably less than polypropylene. While Dynel will bond with either polyester or epoxy resin, in order to realize its special qualities, ONLY a suitable epoxy resin system should be used.

Dynel fabric is relatively lightweight (about half that of comparable fiberglass cloth), non-allergenic, and non-irritating in handling or sanding (although the epoxy resins required may negate this quality to a certain extent for some users). The material wets out easily and rapidly since the weave is much more open than most other sheathing materials, and this allows air to quickly escape. It also conforms more readily to shapes, corners, and contours than does fiberglass cloth, as it can stretch. Dynel is usually used in 4-ounce per square yard weight available by the running yard 39" wide.

In fact, because of the ease of application to difficult contours, Dynel is said to make sheathing of lapstrake or "clinker" type hulls more practical, as the material does not pull away from inside and outside corners and form air bubbles like fiberglass does. This is not necessarily meant as a recommendation that such a practice is guaranteed to work; it just means that Dynel probably has the best chances of success in attempting to sheath a type of hull that seldom yields successful results in sheathing applications due to the inevitable movement inherent in this form of hull construction.

Even though epoxy resins are recommended, for best results each user is advised to make a sample text panel using his choice of resin system to better learn how to handle the materials, and also to subject the test panel to any test conditions that the final product will be required to endure in order to prove the sheathing method, especially in difficult or questionable applications.

Dynel has suffered in the marketplace for many of the same reasons as have polypropylene fabrics. Primarily, there is no need for the material in molded fiberglass boat construction. Hence the market is limited to sheathing work and thus the product is not as readily available.

Another problem that Dynel was hard pressed to overcome during the 60's was a bad, but undeserved, reputation resulting from applications made over old planked hulls using rigid polyester resins, about the only resins available at the time. The expansion and contraction of the planking soon caused the material to crack and split due to the lack of flexibility in the resin, thereby preventing the flexible strength qualities of the fabric from coming into effect.

While some users have attributed the failure of the material to the actual weave pattern of the cloth and not to any inherent weakness of the fibers, Dynel became known as "notch sensitive"; that is, it cracked and split, especially along the seams. Of course, on more stable substrates such as plywood, and when proper epoxy resins are used, these problems don't occur.

WHERE TO USE DYNEL

Dynel fabric overlay can be used just about anywhere fiberglass is used, and is perhaps better for some applications, such as on lapstrake hulls described previously. On conventionally planked hulls ("plank-on-frame" types), Dynel can be used also,

but the highest elongation epoxy resin systems are advised and at least two layers of cloth are recommended. Alternately, a narrow tape can be used over the joints, with a layer of fabric applied over this and the entire hull. It should be stressed that such a hull should be structurally sound in the first place; don't expect such an application to resurrect an unsound hull.

Probably the best success with Dynel, as with other sheathing materials, has been over plywood, cold-molded, or other dimensionally stable surfaces where expansion and contraction, especially at joints, is minimal. The material can also be applied over a surface that has already been sheathed with fiberglass in order to increase the toughness and abrasion resistance. While such a covering would involve more effort and expense, it should yield the ultimate in protection, and would be especially valuable for workboat use.

HOW TO USE DYNEL

Surfaces to be covered with Dynel are prepared as if they were to be covered with fiberglass cloth. Either the wet or dry methods of application can be used although some users recommend a uniform thin coat of resin be applied initially to the surface.

Using the dry method over hulls, the material is laid in position and stapled or tacked along the edges as close as an inch or two in contoured areas, then stretched somewhat to prevent wrinkles. The overhanging edges are then trimmed off. Where overlaps occur, these should be at least 2", and preferably 4". Such overlaps will require feathering at the edge just as with fiberglass materials.

While Dynel will conform to corners better than fiberglass or even polypropylene, it is best to provide some radius to edges and inside corners if only for durability. The material can then be wetted out in the normal manner, with staples and tacks removed before the resin sets up.

With the wet method, the surface is coated with a thin layer of resin using a roller or squeegee to make it uniform. The material, which should have been previously fitted and rolled onto a tube or dowel, is then unrolled into place and smoothed out. When the fabric is wrinkle-free and tight to the surface, a top coat of resin is applied to thoroughly wet out the fabric.

With either the wet or dry method, excess resin should be worked out since a resin-rich laminate tends to be rigid and subject to cracking. Then let the resin cure per the manufacturer's instructions; do NOT attempt to speed the curing cycle in any way since this will promote shrinking, and cracking may occur.

One problem must be kept in mind, however, regarding Dynel. Although it is lightweight by itself, it is a highly absorbent fabric and this causes the fabric to virtually double in thickness once wetted out; it absorbs considerably more resin than either fiberglass or polypropylene fabrics made up from monofilament fibers.

One way to limit absorption is to overlay the sheathing with cellophane or Mylar film and squeegee over this to remove excess resin. Even still, such a sheathing will be about twice as thick as either 4-ounce polypropylene or 10-ounce fiberglass. If overlay film is not used over the surface, the short staple fibers tend to not lay flat to the surface once the resin cures, leaving a rather rough surface. It is this quality that makes Dynel an ideal non-skid deck covering, but one not usually desirable for hull surfaces.

For a sheathing application using two layers, repeat the lay-up process, but sand out sags and rough spots between coats. Overlaps at joints in this method need not be made, but instead use butt joints staggered between layers so they do not occur at the same point. One problem with overlapped areas is that the extra buildup of resin can increase the rigidity at these areas, making such areas more susceptible to cracking. Then too, because of the highly absorbent quality of Dynel, such a covering would tend to be heavy.

To finish the job, cut away remaining untrimmed edges, and sand and feather all laps and edges. Fine sand all surfaces smooth as required, but be careful not to sand too deeply when sanding the first coat as this can damage the weave of the fabric. Sanding Dynel presents some difficulty, however. Because of its superior abrasion resistance and less-than-smooth surface resulting from the fibers as previously noted, any smoothing effect occurs slowly while sanding and the work can be tedious.

In any case, after sanding, another coat of resin will seal any exposed fibers, and a final coat can be used for a hard, smooth surface which can be finish sanded and painted in the normal manner.

For lapstrake hulls, the material is fitted first and stapled or tacked in position, or fitted and then removed, so that either the wet or dry method can be used. However, it would seem easiest to have the material in place first and then wet it out in this application. As with polypropylene, the light weight of the fabric can cause it to float if too much resin is used. Therefore use only enough resin to bond and saturate the cloth. Use a stiff brush to push the saturated fabric into the inside corners of the strakes and then make a final pass with a small roller to insure a tight bond and thorough saturation. Be sure to remove excess resin as noted above. Keep in mind that applying a sheathing to any lapstrake boat will require deft handling and the ultimate in organization, yet results will always be questionable.

For non-skid decking surfaces, the material should be butted at joints; NOT lapped. Apply the fabric using the dry method, but squeegee and scrape off all excess resin so that the fabric is thoroughly saturated, but NOT totally filled and covered with resin.

Do NOT sand the surface. The weave of the fabric is largely what imparts the desired non-skid qualities. No fill or finish coats of resin are required.

When all things are considered, the best use of Dynel appears to be on deck coverings or perhaps workboat sheathing applications where its qualities of toughness and high abrasion resistance may be more important than a smooth, yacht-like surface, which is harder to achieve with Dynel than with other sheathing materials. Also, cost can be a limiting factor because epoxy resins should be considered essential and more resin tends to be used. Attempting to locate a supplier may be difficult without going through mail order firms.

CHAPTER 12   Arabol Glue & Fabric Sheathing

Arabol is probably one of the best kept secrets in boat sheathing materials and processes. It certainly deserves much more exposure than it has received. Arabol is the trade name of a Borden Chemical Company product ordinarily used as a lagging adhesive and coating for thermal insulation. Basically, it is almost identical to ordinary white polyvinyl glue, but modified somewhat to give some additional physical properties, such as better rot and mildew resistance. Borden distributes the material to other firms who market it for various purposes under other names, such as Thorpe "Easy Deck".

Borden refers to the material as a "synthetic plasticized resin emulsion" that dries to a white semi-gloss surface that's easy to clean, fire retardant, and resistant to steam, water, humidity, vermin, and mildew. The resin is virtually odor free, water soluble before curing, and non-flammable. The resin weighs about 12 lbs. per gallon, has a shelf life of about 6 months, and can be damaged by freezing. Although it can be diluted with water, this is seldom done in a sheathing application. Clean up, however, is with soap and water and the material is not hazardous to use.

How did Arabol find its way to the boating field? This is still much a mystery since promotional literature or advertising is virtually non-existent. It seems most hear of the product by word-of-mouth. Thus what follows regarding the use of the material is based on limited experience and feedback from those who have used it.

WHERE IS ARABOL USED?

Basically, Arabol is used in combination with some fabric to provide an overlay for surface protection. The surface is coated with Arabol glue, the fabric placed over the wet glue surface, and allowed to dry, and then successive coats of glue are used over this until the desired surface is obtained. In effect, the Arabol bonds the sheathing material in place and fills the weave, but does not necessarily wet it out in the same manner as does resin with fiberglass.

Just about any fabric can be used with Arabol, including fiberglass cloth and woven rovings, Vectra, Dynel, nylon, muslin, canvas, and burlap. Where the material used is prone to shrinkage, joints should be overlapped. However, other materials which don't shrink can be butt joined. While the product is water soluble in liquid form, it dries to a hard, highly water-resistant coating.

Places where Arabol together with one of the above fabrics can be used include boat decks, cockpit soles, cabin tops and sides, bulkhead coverings, transom steps, gangways, floats, piers, diving boards, swimming pool borders, or any other area where great wear resistance, durability, and water resistance are important. Some have even used the material by itself mixed with ordinary water-based paints for coating stucco-covered buildings subject to extreme weather exposure conditions that lead to failures with other paint systems.

While the Arabol surface is not shiny,

glossy, or otherwise "yachtlike", it does offer a smooth, durable, easy-to-maintain, and weathertight seal coating to all exposed surfaces capable of accepting the bond of the glue. There is no need to paint the Arabol surface, although this can be done. The glue can be tinted with an ordinary waterbase paint pigment and thereby eliminate the need for an undercoat. While specific paint recommendations do not exist, and perhaps a test should be made first if in doubt, most paint types have been used, including waterbased types.

While the Arabol glue is classed as "water resistant", it is not totally waterproof and not recommended as a hull sheathing material or replacement for other materials discussed in this book. However, Arabol is relatively cheap in comparison to polyester or epoxy resins, plus the fabric used can be inexpensive as well. For these reasons, it is often used in workboat conditions. The material requires no special conditions for use, it's hazard-free, and virtually foolproof. The main problem is finding some to buy.

HOW TO USE ARABOL

When using one of the previously noted materials with Arabol, it should be determined if it will shrink in the process. Any cotton material will probably shrink, but many fabrics are either pre-shrunk or are synthetic products which don't shrink. Burlap made from jute or hemp has been used without shrinkage problems, as is the case with fiberglass, nylon, Vectra, and Dynel; but if in doubt, check the fabric with some water. Joints in non-shrinking materials can be butted, but for those which require a lap due to shrinkage, another technique is called for to make lap joints, as will be discussed.

The first step is to prepare the surface, which in most experiences has been wood, although the glue can be used on concrete and stucco with good adhesion. Bonds to other materials such as fiberglass or metals may be questionable. The glue can be applied directly over previously painted surfaces or bare wood as long as all grease and oil have been removed, along with any loose, peeling paint. It can also be applied directly over previously applied canvas covered areas without removing the old material if it has a good bond, although it is a good idea to rough sand any questionable surface first. Keep in mind that the bond of the Arabol will only be as good over previously coated or sheathed surfaces as is the bond of the underlying material.

Precut the material to be used to fit the desired area. If shrinkage is expected, allow 2" on all sides, plus 2" at overlaps. An overlap of an inch or so is often incorporated even with materials that do not shrink just as it was done in the past on cabin tops when glue and canvas were used; some prefer this joint on cabin tops but it is not necessary for keeping out water. Tacking of the fabric in position is not required other than to hold the material in place.

An area of about 10 to 15 square feet is about all that can be done at a time as the Arabol tends to skim over (depending on the ambient temperatures). Don't try to apply the glue at temperatures near freezing as it will not dry properly. Temperatures above 55° to 60° are preferable. Spread the Arabol onto the surface right from the can with a brush using a heavy coating without thinning. For thin fabric materials, less can be used, while heavier materials might take more. In any case, follow the instructions provided with the product.

Lay the material over the glue-coated surface and spread out creases and wrinkles using your hands. Total saturation of the fabric is NOT necessary nor a requirement. This first coat is to just bond the fabric to the surface. If desired, a squeegee can be used to spread out the fabric, pressing hard to work the glue around and into the fabric.

As each section is done, continue working until all the area is covered with the fabric and the initial coating of glue. There is no reason to stop. After application, let the area dry one day or at least overnight. Clean up with ordinary water as long as the glue has not set up hard.

If the material being used will shrink, a different technique is called for to get tight fitting butt joints. Apply one panel of fabric at a time letting it set up fairly hard before going onto the next one, thereby giving the material time to shrink. Then fit the next panel, allowing it to overlap the initial panel by 2".

Place a strip of wax paper on the edge of the joint of the initial panel and then apply glue on the surface where the next panel will go. Place the panel of fabric over the fresh glue letting it overlap onto the wax paper. Then the material will shrink, and after it does, cut down the joint with a utility knife just before the glue sets up. Push the fabric down flush with the surface of the previously applied panel and pull the scrap away along with the wax paper. If carefully cut, a tight, flush butt joint will result even though the fabric may shrink.

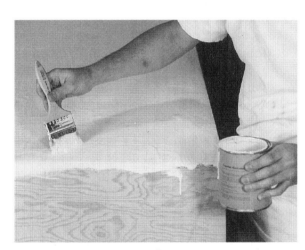

a

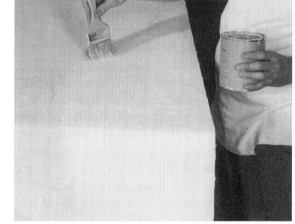

b

TEST PANEL—APPLYING AN ARABOL OVERLAY

Applying an ARABOL overlay is easy. The first coat is brushed onto the surface (a). The fabric is laid onto the wet surface, smoothed out, and allowed to set overnight. The next coat of ARABOL is applied directly over the first coat (b). This coat as well as all successive coats are thinned with approximately 25% water or as specified by the manufacturer. Note how the fresh coat appears much whiter than the dry first coat. The surface can be built up with any number of coats as required to suit the fabric used. This test panel surface was covered with burlap and provided an interesting textured surface which was hard and durable when completed (c).

For the next coats of glue, THIN THE PRODUCT WITH 25% FRESH WATER. You can apply as many coats of Arabol as you wish, but no less than two coats after the initial one are recommended. Let the glue dry for at least four hours between coats. Each coat will dry hard, but there may be some nubs or gritty spots with some fabrics. These can be knocked off with light sanding using a fairly coarse (e.g., #80 grit) sandpaper. Machine sanding is not recommended as the paper will rapidly gum up, be stubborn to sand, and you may risk gouging the material.

With some fabrics such as burlap, tiny "air pits" or craters may form when brushing on the glue or thin areas may appear. These are no problem and can be corrected by just putting on another coat.

For a non-skid deck, burlap is ideal, or you can sprinkle a non-skid compound or ordinary sand onto the next-to-the-last coat. Let the glue dry, brush off the excess, and then apply the final coat. Painting is not required unless desired. While the material goes on white, it dries to a pleasing off-white color that is uniform and suitable for boat work in many applications. If painting is not desired, but a color is, it is recommended that the pigment be added to ALL coats.

How much Arabol will you need? It's impossible to determine as so many different fabrics can be used, plus it all depends on how many coats are used. On ordinary burlap, one gallon will cover about 35 to 40 square feet using four coats. Naturally, thinner and finer woven fabrics will take less, while coarser fabrics will take more.

For previously applied Arabol surfaces that need restoring, all that is required is to clean the area and apply additional coats directly over the old surface (assuming that the surface is not covered with paint or other coatings that are in poor shape or peeling. Some suppliers of the product recommend that old coatings of the glue be softened slightly with a recommended or proprietary solvent to assure a good bond.

How does Arabol stand up in use? In test panels done in preparation for this book, an informal peel test was made by grasping the edge of the coated and cured burlap, and pulling it away from the bare plywood surface. It was difficult to do, but the piece of glue-saturated fabric that was removed took a lot of plywood and glue with it, indicating a good bond. The layer that came off was just like a tough fabric-backed vinyl covering.

Over the years, much feedback has been received, including reports about Arabol used on boat transom steps, docks, piers, gangways, floats and other areas under tremendous foot traffic, sand, gasoline, and water. This is not to mention numerous successful applications on decks and cabin tops. So far no reports of failure, either in use or in application, have been received. For maintenance, all that's usually required is an occasional recoating. For a sheathing that adds only about 3 ounces per square foot using burlap that is easy and inexpensive to apply, Arabol may be the right solution.

Rapid advancements in technology have increased the general level of awareness as to what is "state-of-the-art" at any given moment, and those interested in boats are quick to embrace the latest developments in what has popularly become known as "high-tech" materials. Because of the astounding qualities inherent in some of these new materials, including high prices, they have become known as "exotic" materials.

Two such materials are aramid fiber (better known as "Kevlar", a DuPont product), and carbon fiber (also known as "graphite" fiber). While these two high-strength products (both are stronger than steel or aluminum pound-for-pound) are becoming more commonly used in an ever-increasing array of products, do they have a place in sheathing applications? Let's look them over one at a time and see.

KEVLAR

There is no doubt that Kevlar is a super fiber. It is 2½ times as strong, and up to 3 times stiffer than "E"-glass, and only 43% of the density of fiberglass. It's more durable than fiberglass regarding resistance to damage, vibration, and crack propagation. It has excellent impact resistance. The fibers are woven into fabrics much like fiberglass, which do not require any special finish treatment as does fiberglass. Since Kevlar exists in fabric form, it would seem to be an ideal sheathing material. However, there are problems.

The most important limitation in sheathing applications with Kevlar is that it has only fair abrasion resistance, which as one should know by this time, is a major prerequisite of a sheathing material. Abrade this material and there is an immediate loss of strength. Furthermore, although Kevlar is much stronger than fiberglass in tension, it is not as strong in bending, and about half the strength of fiberglass in compression. While you could sheathe with Kevlar to improve impact strength, it would be recommended to clad this with fiberglass or comparable material for abrasion resistance and to permit fairing or sanding.

Compressive behavior of Kevlar is quite different from fiberglass. Where a compressive failure in a fiberglass laminate is abrupt and catastrophic, but at a high load, in a Kevlar laminate, a compressive failure resembles that of a ductile metal; in other words, it tends to bend or dent. While this may seem to be an asset, such compressive failures in Kevlar laminates occur at relatively low stress levels, thereby causing resin failure through crazing and delamination.

This weakness can be overcome, or at least somewhat compensated for, in a couple of ways. First, the Kevlar layer can be covered with another more suitable material, such as fiberglass. However, in a sheathing situation where strength is secondary, this would be costly and add unnecessary weight, although localized reinforcing, such as at seams could be handled in this manner. Second, there are "hybrid" fabrics available consisting of fiberglass and/or carbon fiber to compensate for the weaknesses of Kevlar, but these would serve little purpose in sheathings also.

Still there are other problems with Kevlar. The material is sensitive to ultraviolet light and should not be used in direct sunlight without the surface being protected by resin containing pigments, or by other protective coatings such as paint or UV-inhibited coatings. Unlike fiberglass and other sheathing materials, Kevlar does not become translucent when wetted out with resin; it retains its yellow cast. This can not only be unattractive (making it impractical for clear coatings), but it makes it difficult (at least for the amateur) to tell if the material is properly and totally saturated with resin.

Other handling difficulties present themselves. Because of its strength, Kevlar is very difficult to cut, both in bare fabric and in cured laminate form. Carbide cutting tools are a virtual necessity, and sanding or fairing against a Kevlar surface is virtually impractical; the material just fuzzes up when abraded or sanded. In the raw state, Kevlar fabric should not be folded so that hard creases form; this can lead to abrasions that damage the fibers, causing loss of strength.

Basically, Kevlar is a fabric that was never intended to be bonded to itself. This means that bonding problems can occur between layers of Kevlar, and if such a laminate is desired, alternate between with a thin layer of fiberglass mat. Because fiberglass and Kevlar have about the same 3% tensile elongation, they are compatible with one another in this setting.

Since Kevlar is made without finish agents, it can be used with many different types of resins including polyester, vinylester, and epoxy. However, to realize its high impact resistance and other physical properties in a laminate, vinylester and epoxy resins are usually advised. Even then, tear and peel strength are not as good as with Vectra when each is used alone in a sheathing situation over a wood substrate.

Considering all aspects of Kevlar, the benefits seem to be greatly overshadowed by the negative aspects, at least for sheathing work. Cost of the fabric is many times higher than fiberglass fabrics that would be comparably used, although availability is becoming more common since the material has many other uses.

The fabric is ordinarily called "Kevlar 49" and is available in several weights per square yard, usually in 38" and 50" widths. While localized reinforcement may be a practical use for Kevlar as long as it is clad with a more durable material such as fiberglass, Kevlar has little to recommend it as a general sheathing material.

CARBON FIBER

Carbon fibers are commonly available in the pure fiber form called "tows". These fibers are often bonded with epoxy for localized reinforcement purposes where additional stiffening and strengthening is required. In this application, they have many uses and perform splendidly if applied properly.

Carbon fiber is not quite as strong in specific tensile strength as Kevlar, but it is considerably stronger in compressive strength. However, carbon fiber is very weak in impact strength. Hence, the two materials are sometimes used together in "hybrid" form to compensate for each material's weaknesses. As with Kevlar, however, carbon fiber cannot stand up to abuse without the help of other materials such as fiberglass.

Besides being weak in impact strength, carbon fiber is weak in sheer strength and must therefore be shielded from abrasion. This quality alone rules it out for most sheathing applications. While carbon fibers can be woven either individually or in hybrid form that could conceivably be used for sheathing, the fibers will lose a certain degree of strength when woven, just as all fibers will. Carbon fibers must be kept straight with no wrinkles or kinks if maximum strength is to be realized. Thus, considering the high premium paid for carbon fiber (it's even more costly than Kevlar), it seems a waste to use the material in any woven form that takes the fibers out of a straight orientation.

There is much disagreement as to the resins that are suitable for use with carbon fiber. Technically, polyester, vinylester, and epoxy resins will all wet out the material. However, some feel that in order to realize optimum strength properties, more flexible resins such as vinylester and epoxy are necessary. From a pure bonding standpoint when applying to a substrate material,

epoxy would be the better choice.

Carbon fiber materials are coal black and will appear this way when wetted out with resin, making them impractical for clear coatings. There is some danger to breathing carbon in the air. Unattached fibers can become airborn easily, so a filter mask should be worn when cutting and fabricating with the material. Metals in contact with carbon (graphite) fiber in salt water are highly susceptible to corrosion; such contact must be avoided. In view of the preceding, carbon fiber has even less to recommend it as a sheathing material than Kevlar.

CHAPTER 14

C-FLEX Sheathing System

The C-FLEX Sheathing System is a patented process for applying a fiberglass skin over new or old wooden boats. The primary ingredient in this system is the C-FLEX fiberglass planking material produced by Seeman Fiberglass. Originally, C-FLEX was developed as a "one-off" fiberglass boatbuilding material suitable for amateurs since it eliminated the need for a female mold. The product has been quite successful in this area, and in effect has revolutionized the field of amateur fiberglass boatbuilding.

For those not familiar with the C-FLEX material, it consists of parallel lengthwise rods of fiberglass rovings reinforced with cured polyester resin (they look much like little continuous lengths of fishing poles side by side) alternating with bundles of continuous fiberglass rovings that are not saturated with resin. The whole is held together by crosswise fiberglass fiber stitching.

C-FLEX comes in 12" wide coiled rolls about 3' in diameter. The material contours easily and conforms to compound curves common in both round-bilged and hard-chined hulls. After the C-FLEX is wetted out with polyester resin, it becomes considerably more rigid. Additional layers of fiberglass reinforcing materials are applied over it, forming a homogenous 100% fiberglass laminate, the strength, stiffness, and weight of which varies with the composition of the materials used.

IS THE C-FLEX SHEATHING SYSTEM FOR YOU?

While advertised as a sheathing system for both new and old wooden boats, the most likely application is for older boats, especially those of plank-on-frame type. While called a sheathing system, this requires some definition of terms. A sheathing system as such merely protects the hull, and any added structural value is incidental. However, in the C-FLEX system, there is the promise of more. To quote the literature, the system " . . . . covers the hull with a high-strength skin . . . . that will greatly increase the life and strength of the boat."

The implication to many might be that an old wood boat can be rejuvenated with the application of this sheathing system and restore the structural strength of the hull in the process. In effect, one is building a new fiberglass "shell" of some structural value on the outside of the wood boat that is much more than a simple sheathing intended merely to protect.

As the system is used, there is some structural function. However, it should not be construed that there is enough structural value in the system to resurrect a boat that is filled with rot, or one that is structurally falling apart, or one that is racked out of shape from age and may be unsafe as a result. It is up to each user to assess his boat to determine if it is sound enough for this system. If in doubt, the advice of the manufacturers of the system should be sought, or consult with a suitable expert such as a marine surveyor.

A prime consideration is the cost involved and whether your boat is worth the expense, not to mention the work. As will be described, several materials are involved in the process and they are not especially cheap. In fact, after adding up the costs, and looking at the work involved, some may feel that it would be better to take the money and put it into another boat, especially if they can cash in on whatever resale value their present boat may have.

However, cost considerations may be secondary in some cases. For example, the boat you want to sheathe with this system may be everything you want in a boat, or it may be equipped in such a manner that another suitable boat may not be practical, or the boat may be a "classic" of some type that without the treatment may wind up on the scrap heap. Then again, you may be emotionally attached to your boat and just want to extend its life or preserve it no matter what the cost or expense. In these cases, the C-FLEX Sheathing System may be for you.

HOW IT WORKS

The C-FLEX Sheathing System involves both chemically bonding and mechanically fastening the C-FLEX to the wooden boat hull. The C-FLEX is applied vertically from gunwale to keel, at least on round-bilged boats. No specific instructions are given for hard-chine hulls regarding directional orientation of the C-FLEX, but part of the principle of the system is to use the strength of the C-FLEX to its best advantage to minimize hull movement, and this is done by placing the C-FLEX perpendicular to the wood planks on wood plank-on-frame boats. However, on hard-chine boats, the joint at the chine between the C-FLEX strips

would require considerable extra build-up of fiberglass to equal the strength of the C-FLEX lost because of the break at this junction.

The mechanical fastening of the C-FLEX is done with heavy bronze staples, while the chemical bond is done by bedding the C-FLEX in an elastomeric adhesive applied to the hull. The C-FLEX is then saturated with resin and covered with layers of fiberglass materials such as mat and woven roving. The results should be protection against rot and marine parasites, increased strength and longevity, and lower maintenance (no more caulking of planking seams). In effect, a fiberglass hull of sorts is made consisting of a wood "framework". Other potential advantages of the system include elimination of hogging when hauling the boat, an increase in hull stiffness, absence of working and creaking, and dry bilges.

However, if your boat has rot, simply adding any sheathing will not eliminate it, or stop its progress, nor will adding a sheathing to the outside of the hull necessarily prevent rot in the future. As long as conditions which led to the rot are not controlled, and rotted members repaired or replaced, rot can still occur in the wood structure even if the boat is sheathed on the outside. One of the prime sources for rot is leaky decks allowing fresh water to enter from above where the sheathing is not located. If humidity and temperature conditions are suitable, and the rot spores exist in poorly ventilated spaces, rot will still proceed.

THE MATERIALS

In addition to the C-FLEX and bronze staples already described, the adhesive recommended to bond it to the wood is a moisture-cured elastomeric polyurethane product developed for marine use. This adhesive bonds well to both wood and the

USING THE C-FLEX SHEATHING SYSTEM

This series of photos shows the procedures of using the C-FLEX Sheathing System over an older wood planked boat (a). Note that the surface has been prepared with all paint removed, repairs made as necessary, and appendages (such as the rub rail) removed. Next the adhesive is applied as in (b) and (c), followed by the C-FLEX. Note the thin temporary battens and permanent staples at intermediate points used to hold the C-FLEX in place as shown by (d) and (e).

Once the C-FLEX is applied, it is wetted out with resin as in (f). This is followed with a laminate starting out with at least one layer of mat (g). Note how the workers are handling the inside corner along the skeg. After the laminate has been applied over the C-FLEX, resin filler coats are applied as in (h) for final sanding and fairing. The completed job in (i) and (j) shows a boat that has a new lease on life, with all the advantages offered by fiberglass hulls.

a

b

c

d

e

f

g

h

i

j

C-FLEX. It will also bond to wet wood, treated wood, and virtually all types of wood used for boat planking. Being elastomeric, it can stretch and compress without breaking the bond, and this is essential in preventing delamination of the sheathing skin from the hull.

An isophthalic polyester laminating resin is recommended to wet out both the C-FLEX and the fiberglass materials applied over it. The fiberglass surface is smoothed out using a fairing compound made up from polyester resin, industrial talc, and glass microspheres.

HULL PREPARATION

It is not necessary to turn the boat over, although this can be done if desired. In fact, the system is ideal for larger boats which cannot practically be turned over and must remain upright. Pick a worksite that will remain dry, and if working indoors is not practical, use plastic sheeting to cover the materials and the boat in case it rains or dew is a possibility. Plastic sheeting can be attached along the sheer of the boat and draped over the work surfaces if necessary.

Remove all hull appendages such as rub rails, guards, thru-hull fittings, chainplates, rudder fittings, etc. All paint should be removed. This can be done by sandblasting, however this must be done with care to prevent damaging the wood planking. Sandblasting leaves a rough texture that actually increases bond quality. Otherwise sanding with a coarse (#16 to #24 grit) paper is another alternative.

Check the quality of the seams, and if they are tight with solid wood each side, leave them alone. Any weak or rotten planks should be replaced, and refastening should be done as required. Patch all holes and do any fairing work required to keep the surface uniform. If the fiberglass will lap onto the deck (a good idea in most cases), prepare this area accordingly.

APPLICATION

The one-part adhesive is applied with a wide notched trowel having ¼" teeth, held at a 45–60° angle, usually starting vertically amidships. In tighter areas, use a putty knife. The adhesive allows about a 4 hour working time before it begins to set up. Warmer temperatures make the adhesive easier to spread, however, it is advisable to work in the shade as much as possible.

C-FLEX is applied directly over the uncured adhesive progressively after several square feet of adhesive are applied, rather than applying adhesive to all surfaces first and then applying the C-FLEX after. Don't try to do this job alone. Several people are best, one applying the adhesive, and at least two cutting, fitting, and applying the C-FLEX close behind.

The adhesive must be squeezed up into the C-FLEX. This can be done by small wood battens temporarily stapled closely across the C-FLEX, and these also hold the material in place. The C-FLEX is then permanently stapled to the hull using about 12 bronze staples per square foot of C-FLEX.

Measure from the deck edge to the bottom of the keel along the girth and cut the lengths of C-FLEX somewhat oversize. Do not overlap the C-FLEX strips, and keep them as fair and flat against the surface as possible. Clean excess adhesive from between the strips. Allow the adhesive to cure (about 24 hours is customary), covering the surfaces with plastic if necessary to keep moisture from settling on the C-FLEX.

Remove the temporary battens and their staples after the adhesive cures, and wet out the C-FLEX with a general purpose polyester laminating resin. Coat an area initially, then move onto an adjacent area. Check the initial area a short while later and recoat again. Work several sections in this manner since the C-FLEX takes a while to wet out. Use only enough resin as is necessary to saturate the C-FLEX (you will begin to see the color of the adhesive through the C-FLEX as it becomes saturated).

Trim any long edges of the C-FLEX with an abrasive cut-off disc or other suitable tool after curing. Use a disc sander to knock down any high spots and grind any edges to a slight radius so the mat to be applied will conform readily. If necessary, a resin putty filler can be used to do any minor fairing and filling that may be needed at this time.

LAMINATE BUILD-UP

At least two layers of fiberglass chopped strand mat are used over the C-FLEX; preferably 1½-ounce weight per layer for a 3-ounce total weight. More laminate may be required depending on several factors, and the user should contact the supplier for their recommendations in this regard. If additional laminate is required, use alternating layers of mat and woven roving for a better interlaminar bond, rather than using only layers of woven roving. Note, however, that each layer, while making a stronger shell, will add weight.

The layers of fiberglass reinforcement will ordinarily require lapping onto the deck edge, across the keel centerline, stem, and other similar junctions for continuity of strength. The application of the laminate once the C-FLEX is on, as well as fairing and finishing techniques, are basically the same as those used in "one-off" fiberglass boatbuilding rather than the sheathing procedures covered in this book. Such information is available in the book, "FIBERGLASS BOATBUILDING FOR AMATEURS", by the author.

GLOSSARY

ACCELERATOR – Material used in conjunction with a catalyst to produce and hasten the internal heat reaction for cure of polyester resin. The accelerator used in most polyester resins for boat work is cobalt napthanate, usually referred to as "cobalt".

ACETONE – A highly flammable and toxic cleaning fluid solvent used to remove uncured resin from tools and clothing. Will attack rayon and Dacron.

ACTIVATOR – See **ACCELERATOR**

AIR BUBBLES – Entrapment of air particles (whether small or large) in resin or a fiberglass laminate caused by improper mixing of the resin, improper wetting out of a laminate, forming fiberglass around abrupt corners, etc. Air bubbles weaken the bond in a fiberglass laminate and its strength, and make a laminate more permeable by moisture.

AIR-INHIBITED RESIN – A resin which will not completely cure or "set up" in the presence of air. Polyester resin which does not contain wax is classed as "air-inhibited". Also called "laminating" resin.

"ARABOL" – Tradename for a synthetic plasticized resin similar to white polyvinyl glue and frequently used as a lagging adhesive. The product can also be used with various fabrics for covering surfaces, much like fiberglass materials with resin.

BINDER – A bonding agent used to adhere fibers in the manufacturing of fiberglass materials, especially mat.

BLUSH – A defect that shows up as a discoloration or blotchy surface on a resin coated surface, usually caused by moisture introduced during the curing cycle, or by putting the boat in the water prior to total cure. Amine blush is a thin waxy-like build-up resulting from the completed cure of certain epoxy resins; it is water-soluble and harmless.

BOND – The adhesion between two materials. Also, to attach materials together by means of an adhesive agent or glue.

BUTT JOINT – A joint made by positioning materials together end-to-end or side-by-side without any overlap.

CATALYST – Material added to polyester resin to make it cure rapidly by oxidizing an accelerator. This causes the heat which in turn cures the resin. The common catalyst for polyester resins used in boat work is MEK peroxide.

CHOPPER GUN – A special spray gun used for spray-up laminates which chops fiberglass rovings into pre-determined lengths and deposits them together with catalyzed resin at the same time onto a surface such as a mold.

CLOTH – A woven fabric made from fine yarns of fiberglass or similar material.

COMPOSITE – Type of construction using two or more different materials together, such as fiberglass and resin.

CRATERING – A surface defect consisting of pinholes or pockmarks (sometimes called "fisheyes" also).

CRAZING – Hairline cracks either within a laminate or on the surface, caused by (among other things) stresses generated by excessive heat during cure, impact, and flexing.

CURE – The changing of the liquid resin to a solid state of maximum hardness. The technical term is "polymerization".

CURE TIME – The time required for the liquid resin to reach a point when it is hard enough to have other processes performed with it or on it, such as sanding. Also, the time it takes a resin to reach a state when it is no longer "tacky" or "sticky". Technically, it is the time required for the resin to reach a "polymerized state" after a catalyst or hardener has been added.

DELAMINATION – Separation or failure of the bond in laminate layers from each other or from a substrate material.

DIMENSIONAL STABILITY – The ability to retain constant shape and size, as opposed to "stretching" and "shrinking".

DRAPEABILITY – The ability of a fiberglass or similar material to conform to contours, corners, and shapes when saturated with resin.

DRY SPOT – Area of low resin content in a sheathing composite or laminate. Also referred to as a "resin starved" area.

"DYNEL" – Tradename for modacrylic fiber which is spun or woven into various fabrics that can be used with resin for sheathing purposes.

EPOXY RESIN – Thermosetting resins in boat work of a two-part type (resin and hardener), that when combined, cure and form an extremely tough, strong plastic product that will adhere tenaciously to many materials with negligible shrinkage and moisture absorption.

EXOTHERMIC HEAT – The heat given off by the resin developed internally during "polymerization", caused by the reaction of the catalyst with the accelerator (in the case of polyester resin), and by the hardener with the resin (in the case of epoxy resin).

FEATHER EDGE – The process of tapering the edge of a resin-saturated fiberglass material to blend with the adjoining surface, as opposed to having an abrupt edge.

FIBERGLASS – Fibers similar to those of other fabrics, but made from glass. Also, the materials made from these fibers. Loosely defines the plastic laminates made with fiberglass and resins.

FILAMENT – A single thread-like fiber, or a number of these fibers, put together in a virtually endless length, and used to make fiberglass yarns and threads.

FILLER – Relatively inert material added to resin to extend the volume, or change or improve the qualities of the resin.

FILLET – A rounded filling on an inside corner or angle forming a concave junction where these two surfaces meet so that air bubbles are not formed in the adjoining laminate.

FINISH – The surface cleaning treatment given to glass fibers or filaments after weaving them into cloth in order to allow resin to flow freely around and adhere to them. The finish determines the quality of adhesion between the glass and the resin, and the ability of a fabric to be wet out readily by the resin.

FIRE-RETARDANT – Resin type which has been formulated with chemicals or additives to reduce or eliminate its tendency to burn when once cured or "polymerized" after the flame source has been removed.

FLEXIBILITY – A qualitative term used to subjectively describe the degree of rigidity of a resin after it cures. Resins are usually described as "flexible", "semi-flexible" ("semi-rigid"), or "rigid". However, a "flexible" resin is not purely flexible nor is a "rigid" resin totally rigid.

GEL/GELATION – The partial cure of resin to a semi-solid or "jelly-like" state.

GEL COAT – A thin decorative and protective surface coat of specially formulated resin (usually polyester) used as a surface covering on parts or hulls made in female molds, usually applied by spray gun.

GEL TIME – The time required to change the liquid resin to a non-flowing gel. Also, the time available for working the resin once it is applied. See also **POT LIFE**.

HAND LAYUP – The building up of fiberglass laminates using manual labor and low pressure techniques within or over a substrate or mold surface.

HARDENER – Although sometimes used interchangeably with the term, catalyst, the hardener is usually considered the catalyst used with epoxy resins (also called part "B").

INHIBITOR – An additive that retards or slows down or prevents a chemical reaction. May be used to extend the shelf life of a resin, or influence gel time and exothermic heat.

ISOPHTHALIC ("ISO") RESIN – Isophthalic acid based polyester resin which has somewhat higher physical and chemical resistant properties than orthophthalic resins, but is still considered a "general purpose" polyester resin.

LAMINATE – A material or composition made from successive layers of sheathing materials bonded together and saturated with resin.

LAMINATION – A layer of material in a laminate.

LAP JOINT – A joint made by positioning one material over another end-to-end or side-by-side as opposed to a butt joint. The joint can consist of two or more layers of material.

LAYUP – The placing of sheathing materials in or on a surface and applying resin to form the completed laminate. Sometimes used interchangeably with the term, laminate.

MAT – A felt-like material of randomly oriented strands or chopped strands of glass fibers held together with a binder.

"M-E-K" – Methylethyl ketone, a solvent sometimes used for cleaning purposes and NOT to be confused with "M-E-K peroxide".

"M-E-K PEROXIDE" – Methylethyl ketone peroxide, the catalyst commonly used for curing polyester resin.

MICROSPHERES – Generic name for hollow lightweight microscopically tiny beads used as a filler material in resins. When mixed with resin, they form what is called a "syntactic foam".

MOLD – An appliance or device used to shape or duplicate a part. When a part is made OVER and around the exterior of the mold, this type of mold is a "male" mold. When the part is made inside the mold surface, this type of mold is called a "female" or "cavity" mold.

MOLD RELEASE – See **PARTING AGENT**

MONOMER – A simple compound capable of polymerization with itself or a compatible resin, while acting as a diluting agent. Styrene is the common monomer used in polyester resin.

NON-AIR-INHIBITED RESIN – A resin which will completely cure or "set up" in the presence of air. Polyester resin which contains wax is classed as "non-air-inhibited". Also called "finishing" resin.

ORTHOPHTHALIC ("ORTHO") RESIN – Orthophthalic acid based polyester resin. Considered a "general purpose" resin of average qualities.

PARTING AGENT – Any material applied to a mold or other surface to prevent resin from sticking to it. Also called "parting film", "release agent", and "mold release". Common materials include wax, polyvinyl alcohol ("PVA"), cellophane, plastic film, Mylar, and plastic laminate products.

PIGMENTS – Coloring additives used to give color to resin much like the addition of pigments to paint.

POLYESTER RESIN – Thermosetting resins which require the addition of a catalyst and accelerator to effect the cure. This type of resin is commonly used in boat work.

POLYMER – The technical word of the end product produced from a monomer.

POLYMERIZATION – The chemical reaction of a monomer, usually from a liquid state to a solid state. See also **CURE**.

POT LIFE – The length of time that a catalyzed resin remains workable while in the container until it must be discarded. Similar to **GEL TIME** except that this refers to the working time once the resin has been applied to a surface.

RELEASE AGENT – See **PARTING AGENT**.

RESIN – A liquid plastic substance used to bond and saturate sheathing materials which polymerizes to form a structural laminate.

RESIN RICH – An area in a laminate where too much resin exists in relation to the reinforcing material. Also referred to as a "resin pocket" or "resin streak".

ROVING – Continuous strands of glass or other fibers grouped together to form an untwisted yarn or rope.

SECONDARY BOND – Subsequent bonding of materials where the initial laminate has cured.

SET UP – Resin which hardens and is basically "cured" is said to have "set up", or polymerized (although a TOTAL cure may not yet have been completed).

SHELF LIFE – The length of time an uncatalyzed resin remains usable while stored in a sealed container.

SIZING – The surface treatment of glass fibers during fiber forming operations which aids in machine manufacture as well as aiding resin compatibility. Sizing is similar to **FINISH** for cloth, but because mats and rovings are not "dirtied" by the weaving process, no finish is required.

SPRAY-UP – A method of fiberglass layup performed with a **CHOPPER GUN** (see also) which cuts and deposits fiberglass rovings and catalyzed resin onto a surface. See also **HAND LAYUP**.

SQUEEGEE – Any tool used to wet out a laminate with a smoothing, spreading, or wiping action, in order to eliminate wrinkles and air entrapment.

STRAND – A bundle of continuous filaments.

STYRENE – The primary monomer ingredient and diluting agent used in polyester resins.

SURFACING AGENT – Material added to polyester resin or used with it to prevent air from reaching the surface so that the resin will cure tack-free. Paraffin wax in a solution of styrene is a common type. PVA also serves this purpose, but it is not mixed with the resin.

SYNTACTIC FOAM – Resin which has been made lower in density, lighter in weight, higher in viscosity, and generally "stretched out" for filling purposes.

TACK – Quality of stickiness of a cured or partially- cured resin surface.

THERMOPLASTIC RESIN – A type of resin which can be repeatedly softened or reformed by the application of heat, and can be rehardened by cooling. This type of resin is not used in boat work.

THERMOSETTING RESIN – A type of resin which will undergo a chemical change from a liquid state as the result of the heat induced by the addition of certain materials. Once it becomes solid, it cannot be reformed by reheating. Polyester and epoxy resins are examples of this type.

THICKENER – Material added to resin to thicken or increase the viscosity so it will not flow as readily. See **FILLER**.

THINNER – Material added to resin in order to thin it or lower its viscosity.

THIXOTROPIC – A quality of some resins to thicken at rest, but become fluid again on agitation and stirring.

"VECTRA" – Trade name for polypropylene fiber that is spun and woven into various fabrics that can be used with resin for sheathing purposes.

VINYLESTER RESIN – A type of polyester resin with improved physical and chemical resistant properties, especially at elevated temperatures, compared to either ortho or iso polyesters.

VISCOSITY – The quality of a liquid's resistance to flow. A more viscous liquid will not flow as easily as one that has less viscosity.

WET OUT – A material which is saturated with resin is said to be "wet out". Also the quality of a material's ability to absorb resin.

WOVEN ROVING – Rovings of fiberglass or comparable materials woven into a coarse, heavy fabric.

YARN – Twisted strand or strands of glass or comparable fibers which can be woven, braided, served, and processed on conventional textile equipment.

INDEX